STUDIES ON THE TESTAMENT OF MOSES

Seminar Papers

edited by

George W. E. Nickelsburg, Jr.

for the

Society of Biblical Literature
Pseudepigrapha Group

SEPTUAGINT AND COGNATE STUDIES, NUMBER FOUR

SOCIETY OF BIBLICAL LITERATURE

1973

Library of Congress Catalog Card Number 73-89039

ISBN 0-89130-167-4 (Formerly 0-88414-029-6)

Copyright © 1973 by the Society of Biblical Literature,
Cambridge, Massachusetts

TABLE OF CONTENTS

Preface	4
Introduction	5
The Date and Provenance of the Testament of Moses *John J. Collins*	15
An Antiochan Date for the Testament of Moses *George W. E. Nickelsburg, Jr.*	33
Some Remaining Traditio-Historical Problems in the Testament of Moses *John J. Collins*	38
The Testament of Moses: Its Content, Its Origin, and Its Attestation in Josephus *Jonathan A. Goldstein*	44
The Assumption of Moses and Jewish History: 4 B.C.–A.D. 48 *David M. Rhoads*	53
Interpreting Israel's History: The Testament of Moses as a Rewriting of Deut 31-34 *Daniel J. Harrington*	59
Summary of Günther Reese, *Die Geschichte Israels in der Auffassung des frühen Judentums*, Ch III *Daniel J. Harrington*	69
The Assumption of Moses as a Testament *Anitra Bingham Kolenkow*	71
The Text of Deuteronomy Employed in the Testament of Moses *Ralph W. Klein*	78
On the Non-Relationship of the Testament of Moses to the Targumim *Sheldon R. Isenberg*	79
The Figure of Moses in the Testament of Moses *David L. Tiede*	86
Samaritan Traditions on the Death of Moses *James D. Purvis*	93
Three Armenian Accounts of the Death of Moses *Michael E. Stone*	118
The Ascension of Moses and the Heavenly Jerusalem *Harold W. Attridge*	122

PREFACE

The articles in this volume are _working papers_ prepared for the sessions of the Society of Biblical Literature Pseudepigrapha Group, to be held November 8 and 9, 1973, at the Palmer House in Chicago, Illinois, under the chairmanship of Prof. John Strugnell and the undersigned, with Prof. George W. MacRae serving as respondent.

I wish to thank especially Prof. Strugnell, with whom I have worked closely in the preparation of the program and of this volume, and the several contributors, for their willingness to assume the added burden of an assigned paper. Prof. MacRae, who serves as Executive Secretary of the SBL, has been particularly helpful in matters relating to the production of this volume. The Introduction is the responsibility of the editor; however, I have profited to no small degree from conversations with friends and colleagues: John Strugnell, George MacRae, John Collins, Anitra Kolenkow, and Harold Attridge.

George W.E. Nickelsburg, Jr.
School of Religion
University of Iowa
Iowa City, Iowa 52242

INTRODUCTION

The Assumption of Moses is the familiar title of the little document that is the subject of the present volume. It was so identified in 1861 by its first editor, Antonio Ceriani.¹ His identification was based on patristic references to a work known as Ἀνάληψις Μωυσέως, one of which quotes the first chapter of the work we are considering.² In 1897, R.H. Charles argued in detail in his edition and annotated translation that the text was really a testament of Moses, which had been prefixed to the work known as the Assumption of Moses, and that both of them then circulated under the latter title.³ In fact, he observed, the Stichometry of Nicephorus lists in immediate succession a Testament of Moses (Διαθήκη Μωυσέως) and an Assumption of Moses (Ἀνάληψις Μωυσέως). In the present volume, we have adopted Charles' nomenclature.

To the present day, our only text of this work is the Latin ms. published by Ceriani. It is a palimpsest of the fifth century, illegible in places. Its ending, which presumably included a description of Moses' death and burial, has been lost. As Charles has shown, it is a translation of a Greek translation of a Semitic original.⁴ Since 1897, the only major study of the Testament of Moses (hereafter TM) has been an annotated French translation with extended introduction by E.-M. Laperrousaz.⁵ Therefore, the work seemed a natural candidate for study by the Society of Biblical Literature Pseudepigrapha Group.

Legion are the questions which the scholar may address to the Testament of Moses. At an early stage in the preparation for the session of the Pseudepigrapha Group, it was decided to limit such questions to areas in which: (a) modern biblical scholarship in general has raised new and substantive issues; and where (b) new insights call into question some of the older answers to more traditional questions about TM. To that end, paper topics were developed under three headings.

1. Date and Provenance
2. Form and Function
3. Relationship to Parallel Traditions

---

¹Antonio Ceriani, Monumenta sacra et profana, Vol. 1, fasc. 1 (Milan, 1861), pp. 55-64.

²For these quotations, see A.-M. Denis, "Assumptio Mosis," in Apocalypsis Henochi Graeci et Fragmenta Pseudepigraphorum Quae Supersunt Graeca, edd. M. Black and A.-M. Denis. PVTG 3 (Leiden, 1970), pp. 63-67. For the quotation mentioned above, see p. 63.

³R.H. Charles, The Assumption of Moses (London, 1897), pp. xlv-li.

⁴On the original language, see ibid., pp. xxxvi-xlv, and David H. Wallace, "The Semitic Origin of the Assumption of Moses," TZ 11 (1955), 321-28.

⁵E.-M. Laperrousaz, Le Testament de Moïse, Semitica 19 (Paris, 1970). For additional bibliography, see Gerhard Delling, Bibliographie zur Jüdisch-Hellenistischen und Intertestamentarischen Literatur: 1900-1965, TU 106 (Berlin, 1969), pp. 104f.; A.-M. Denis, "Les Fragments Grecs de l'Assumption de Moïse," in Introduction aux Pseudépigraphes Grecs d'Ancien Testament, SVTP 1 (Leiden, 1970), pp. 128-41.

Although the individual papers were construed under one of these headings, in point of fact, a paper in one area may contribute to the discussion in another area.

This introduction is partly an attempt to correlate some of the ways in which the various papers speak to the issues at hand. Where is there substantial agreement? Where are there conflicting conclusions? Moreover, what new issues arise from these papers and the ways in which they touch on one another? What do the papers contribute to our understanding of the broader issues involved in the study of Second Temple Judaism? In all of these matters, I propose only to be suggestive and, hopefully, provocative of a substantial discussion in the actual sessions of the Pseudepigrapha Group.

Date

Since 1897, scholars have almost unanimously accepted Charles' dating of TM to 7-30 C.E.[6] Jacob Licht gave the discussion a new turn in 1961, when he cautiously suggested that the work was composed "slightly earlier than the apocalyptic parts of Daniel" and was interpolated and updated in Herodian times.[7] Licht's hypothesis was followed and built upon in a book by the present writer,[8] but otherwise it has gone largely unnoticed in scholarly discussions of the subject in the past decade.[9] The first paper in this volume, by John Collins, was intended to examine the alternatives in dating in a systematic way, and Collins decides in favor of the Herodian date. However, in his response to my response, he tends to accept the early date. At the same time, he maintains that the setting he originally proposed for the _composition_ of TM is still appropriate to its Herodian redaction. If the conclusions from this interchange are to be accepted, we are confronted with a redactor who must be taken seriously as an author in his own right with a very specific purpose in mind. He is not simply updating an old document.

In the second major paper, Jonathan Goldstein _assumes_ the earlier dating and then suggests that some of the material which now refers to Herodian times may originally have been descriptive of events connected with Antiochus Epiphanes. Apocalyptists, he argues, were conservative when they revised documents. They utilized what they could and interpolated only what was necessary. David Rhoads, while taking note of Licht's article, _assumes_ a date in the first century C.E. He then suggests a setting amid and in opposition to first century revolutionary movements which is quite close to that suggested by Collins.

---

[6]Charles, _Assumption_, pp. lv-lviii. For an exception, see Solomon Zeitlin, "The Assumption of Moses and the Revolt of Bar Kokba," _JQR_ 38 (1947/48), 1-45. See below, p. 16.

[7]Jacob Licht, "Taxo, or the Apocalyptic Doctrine of Vengeance," _JJS_ 12 (1961), 95-103.

[8]George W.E. Nickelsburg, Jr., _Resurrection, Immortality, and Eternal Life in Intertestamental Judaism_, HTS 26 (Cambridge, 1972), pp. 28-31,43-45,97.

[9]Mention of it is missing in G. Reese, thesis cited below, n.16 (1967); K. Haacker, _art. cit._ below, n. 11 (1969), and Laperrousaz, op. cit., above, n. 5.

Provenance

In many ways, this is one of the most difficult questions that we can address to a document, and often it is unanswerable. At least three cautions must be exercized.

1) As Rhoads correctly reminds us, recent finds and modern scholarship have rendered untenable the older and fairly simple schematizations of late Second Temple Judaism. It will no longer do simply to label the author of a document like TM as a Pharisee, a Sadducee, an Essene, or a Zealot--as if these were the only options. For the earlier period, our knowledge is even more sketchy. Thus it would be useful, e.g., (as Collins suggests) to attempt to define more precisely the term "hasidic," as I myself have used it, seeking clarification in documents such as Daniel, some of the earlier parts of Jubilees and Enoch, and 1 and 2 Maccabees.

2) It is not sufficient to observe that TM, e.g., is compatible with the teachings and other contours of a given group. We must ask further whether it conforms closely to what appear to be unique aspects of that group, or, on the other hand, whether it clashes with the basic tenets of another group. In this respect, both Colins and Goldstein have moved with some caution in their conclusions.

3) Finally, we must recognize the spottiness of our knowledge of the period. Today's probability may prove to be tomorrow's misjudgment. The suggestion of an Essene provenance for the composition (or redaction) of TM is not without its irony. Charles rejected this possibility precisely because of the references to temple and sacrifice; for, he noted, the Essenes were excluded from the temple courts and disapproved of animal sacrifices[10] Our increased knowledge regarding the strong priestly character of the Essene movement and of the historical circumstances surrounding the Essene exile from temple and temple sacrifices have put the issue in a totally different light. This can serve as ample warning against facile and final judgments regarding the historical setting of these ancient documents.

Klaus Haacker offers the hypothesis of a Samaritan provenance.[11] The hypothesis is detailed and criticized in the paper by James Purvis.[12] Haacker has mustered an impressive series of parallels from Samaritan sources, but what are the alternative explanations? Purvis suggests that the author of TM may have known an early Samaritan writing (this would presume a late date for TM if we accept Purvis' dating of the Samaritan schism[13]) or (a) Samaritan author(s) may have known TM.[14] Our second observa-

---

[10]Charles, Assumption, pp. liiif.

[11]Klaus Haacker, "Assumptio Mosis: eine samaritanische Schrift?" TZ 25 (1969), 385-405.

[12]See below, pp. 116-17. Cf. also the articles by Collins and Harrington below, pp. 16,59.

[13]James D. Purvis, The Samaritan Pentateuch and the Origin of the Samaritan Sect, HSM 2 (Cambridge, 1968). He sets the date for the schism after Hyrcanus' destruction of the Gerizim temple.

[14]This hypothesis is most consonant with a date for TM before the schism, thus facilitating Samaritan access to the Jewish writing.

tion above must also be considered. Are there any uniquely Samaritan elements (ideas, terminology, etc.) in the parallel Samaritan traditions which are found--or are missing--in TM? Are there any conspicuously un-Samaritan elements in TM? One of the latter suggests itself. Haacker sees in 6:1 a brief reference to Hyrcanus' destruction of the Samaritan temple on Mt. Gerizim (402). But facient facientes impietatem ab sancto sanctitatis is an odd and particularly vague way to refer to such an event, and it is better read as a reference to Hasmonaean activities in the Jerusalem temple, which a Samaritan author would surely not describe in this manner.

Form and Function

What is the "shape" of this work? What is its literary genre? How do its various parts relate to one another? What was its intended purpose or function, its Sitz im Leben? How is it similar to or dissimilar from analogous documents?

1. A Rewriting of Deuteronomy 31-34

That TM purports to retell the events described in Deut 31-34 is obvious enough. Whether, and to what extent terms such as "targum," "midrash," and "haggadah" are applicable here should not divert us from some broader and more significant questions. The text of Deuteronomy provides us with a control by which to ascertain the author's technique. Where, and in what ways does he diverge from the biblical text? Are these divergences accidental or significant? Do they have parallels in contemporary literature? To a large extent, this last question is dealt with in papers listed under our last category.

The elements in Deut 31-34 for which there are counterparts in TM are:

1. The announcement of Moses' death
2. The commissioning of Joshua
3. Commands to preserve the book
4. An extensive revelation of the history of Israel
5. The Blessing of Moses
(6. The death and burial of Moses--presumably in the lost conclusion of TM)

Daniel Harrington has focused on TM's rewriting of the historical material in Deuteronomy. This subject has also been discussed by Günther Reese (see abstract below, pp. 69f.) and Enno Janssen (see pp. 66-68), and since this material is at the heart of TM, it is useful to begin here. As Harrington notes, Deut 28-30 and Deut 32 differ from one another in this significant respect, that in the former, but not in the latter, divine deliverance from the oppressor is preceded by Israel's repentance. This repentance is mentioned in the Deuteronomic traditions in Jub 1 (and, I think, 23:26) and, as Baltzer has shown, in the eschatological sections of the Testaments of the Twelve Patriarchs.[15] Harrington correctly notes that my characterization of Taxo's action as "repentance" is inappropriate (unless one reads 1:18 as a specific reference to Taxo). On the other hand, he notes that the presence of intercessors such as Moses, the unnamed figure in ch. 4, and Taxo represent a departure from the simple pattern of

---

[15] Klaus Baltzer, The Covenant Formulary (E.T.; Philadelphia, 1971), pp. 153-61.

Deut 32. In view of this fact, is it possible that this element may be functioning in the use of the Deuteronomic tradition as an analog or counterpart to repentance? If there is any such correspondence, it is nevertheless necessary to note the unique nuance in TM. Collins has dealt with this question (below, p.42).

Harrington notes the similarity between TM and Josephus' understanding of Deut 32 as a prediction of current events, indeed of events that repeat themselves. Here we may inquire into the function of TM and into its inner logic. Is our author maintaining that Israel's history repeats itself, albeit it in a stepped fashion, from partial to full vindication? Or is he presenting the first cycle of events as paradigmatic, i.e., as a promise that Israel can expect deliverance in the present crisis? This latter view is argued by Reese and, in the present volume, by Anitra Kolenkow, who cites yet other passages in TM.

Finally, other matters relating to the historical materials and to TM's reuse of material from the Blessing of Moses will be discussed below under the category of "apocalyptic."

The transmission and preservation of the book and of the Song of Moses are mentioned several times in Deut 31 (vv. 9-13, 19-22, 24-26, 28-30). Similar statements occur in TM 1:16 and 10:11, but with the common "apocalyptic" nuance that the present book is to be hidden until the end time.

An understandable interest in the historical (read "theological") material in TM has too often diverted attention away from the narrative framework of the book. An exception is Reese, who argues at some length, and persuasively, that the author has interpolated his historical material into an already extant narrative framework.[16] This source looks very much like a typical biblical commissioning scene, albeit with its own emphases and nuances.

Reese offers a suggestion as to why the author has used this Moses-Joshua material as the framework for his discussion of Israel's history (see abstract). Anitra Kolenkow has also focused attention on the framework and emphasized its significance for a proper understanding of the author's purpose and viewpoint.

---

[16]Günther Reese, *Die Geschichte Israels in der Auffassung des frühen Judentums* (Diss. Heidelberg, 1967), pp. 89-93. He notes that while the Moses-Joshua material is the framework for the disclosure of Israel's history, it is quite unrelated to the historical material:

> Die lange Entgegnung Joshuas auf die Rede des Mose geht mit keiner Silbe auf die eben gehörte Geschichtsdarstellung ein, beschäftigt sich dafür ausschliesslich mit den Problemen, die sich daraus ergeben, dass Joshua als der "Nachfolger Moses in diesem Bund" (10,15) eingesetzt werden soll. Und von der Antwort, die Mose darauf gibt (Kap. 12), liessen sich zwar 12,5 und 12,11ff in etwa auf die ganze Geschichtsdarstellung beziehen, aber diese Verse wollen doch in erster Linie eine Antwort auf die zweifelnden Einwände Joshuas in Kap 11, besonders V. 16-19, geben und stehen, zumal eine direkte Bezugnahme auf die Geschichtsdarstellung fehlt, viel eher in Konkurrenz zu ihr, als dass sie auf sie zurückgreifen. So legt sich die Vermutung nahe, dass die Geschichtsdarstellung in eine bereits vorliegende Erzählung eingefügt worden ist. (From p. 90)

Central to this material are: God's foreknowledge regarding history; the Gentiles' ignorance of God's plan and of his continuous presence in Israel; their ignorance of the fact that God will ultimately convict them for their oppression of his people. But we may go further. As Ms. Kolenkow suggests (note 6), the author has in mind the present crisis, in which the Gentiles are threatening the very existence of Israel. Our author maintains that although God allows the Gentiles to punish his people, he will not permit their complete annihilation. The document as a whole takes on the character of a disputation. Moses predicts the course of history, including its consummation in the theophany. When he announces his death, Joshua protests (typical feature of a commissioning here transformed) that without Moses' mediating presence, Israel will be overwhelmed and destroyed. Moses counters with the assurance (again a typical commissioning element) that God has foreseen the course of history including the present and with the promise that Israel will not be annihilated. The extant section concludes with his reassertion of the coming theophany.

The source of these arguments regarding the Gentiles is Deut 32 itself. God has created all the nations including Israel (32:8f.; TM 12:4). The "foolish nation" (32:21) is permitted by God to punish Israel, but it arrogantly miscalculates the situation (32:27-30) and is brought low. The argument is reminiscent of 2 Macc 7:16-19, also based on Deut 32, where, however, the author appears to be issuing a warning to the Gentiles not to misunderstand Israel's situation as an invitation to oppress her.[17] Here our author adds his own nuances regarding foreknowledge (not surprising in an "apocalyptic" document) and God's deceit of the Gentiles, and he uses the material to encourage the persecuted people of God.

2. A Testament

Anitra Kolenkow analyses the significance of TM as a Testament, an example of a common literary genre in the Hellenistic-Jewish world. A natural question arises. Does TM contain a "deathbed" revelation because the author has written a testament or because he has written a paraphrase of the last chapters of Deuteronomy, which contain just such an "ante-mortem" prophecy. But perhaps the question is wrongly put. For whatever reason, our author sets out to rewrite the last chapters of Deuteronomy. What is striking is his delimitation of the material. He begins precisely with the announcement of Moses' death (and presumably ends with his burial) and thus gives his rewriting the character of a testament with all that this might connote with respect to the prophecy contained therein. If Reese is correct in his contention that the author has drawn his narrative framework from a longer, extensive paraphrase of Deuteronomy, the technique is again patent. The author has utilized material from his source that will provide the framework for a testament.

As Ms. Kolenkow indicates, the question of the shape and function of the testament genre (if we may use the term in the singular) is a complex one, and it needs definition. If we are willing to define as a testament any document that describes events in connection with a person's death, we must clearly move beyond Klaus Baltzer's delimitation of the material. And indeed the incipits of certain documents appear to require that we do so.

---

[17] Nickelsburg, Resurrection, pp. 95f.

It appears, then, that the testament genre takes on a number of different shapes and serves various purposes. Without pursuing the matter any further here, it is worth noting that the area promises fruitful results if the right kind of questions are asked.

In her discussion of the term "testament," Ms. Kolenkow speaks of both the giving and the receiving of revelations at the time of death. The distinction ought not be passed over too quickly, and it may provide a handle by which to understand the function of a particular testament. It is one thing to suppose that one _receives_ revelation at the time of death because, for whatever reason, this is a moment of peculiar insight--and those reasons ought to be ascertained and sorted out carefully in each individual case. It is quite another thing, conceivably, to emphasize that the time of death is the occasion for an individual to _pass on_ those insights which he has received at some previous time. Here we have the natural concern at the time of death for the passing on of one's heritage. In some cases, as in the Book of Enoch, the protagonist both passes on revelations received earlier (cf., e.g., 83:2) and is inspired to receive and transmit new revelations (91:1).

The scholarly process has carried us back through our document to a historical setting, a _Sitz im Leben_ and a function. We may now exercise our historical imagination and ask: why a Testament of Moses? The question is a fair one and worth asking. Granting our author's purpose, why did he embody it in a testament of Moses? If we grant the common practice of using the Deuteronomic material as an explanation of one's current troubles (if not as a promise of deliverance from those troubles)--and there seems to be some evidence for this supposition--then, given the literary device of pseudepigraphy, it seems almost natural that someone in the supposed situation would flesh out the Deuteronomic historical pattern in terms of present events and present the whole in the form of a pseudepigraphic testament of the author of Deuteronomy. In fact, a Testament of Moses seems at least as likely as a pseudonymous historical apocalypse to and through Daniel or Enoch.

3. Apocalypse/Apocalyptic

We cannot leave the form-critical question without touching on the fact that TM is generally regarded as in some sense "apocalyptic," if not as an apocalypse.[18] The judgment needs to be re-examined in the light of recent discussions of the nature of apocalyptic. In what sense is the term appropriate and, indeed, meaningful?

We may claim that TM is an apocalypse in that it purports to be a revelation of events yet to come. But so does its prototype, the Song of Moses, which few, if any, would dub an apocalypse. One might maintain that TM cites events which are more specific or detailed, but perhaps our ignorance of the particular events alluded to in Deut 32 leads us to make more of this distinction than actually exists. There may be some merit, from a form-critical view point, in seeing TM in analogy to an apocalypse such as Dan 10-12, which in certain important respects takes the

---

[18] E.g., it is included among the "apocalyptic" literature by H.H. Rowley, _The Relevance of Apocalyptic_ (Rev. ed.; New York, 1964), pp. 106-110; and D.S. Russell, _The Method and Message of Jewish Apocalyptic_ (Philadelphia, 1964), pp. 58f.

form of an extended commissioning scene. That particular possibility would have to be considered in the light of other observations made above regarding the material concerning Joshua's commissioning. We must take care not to assign multiple functions to given elements.

Perhaps more profitably, the discussion should focus on the question: In what sense is the theology of TM "apocalyptic"? For our present purposes, we need not delay over the many definitions of that term and the many ways in which scholars have characterized apocalyptic. For the purpose of catalyzing discussion, we may briefly characterize the book's eschatology, indicating points of continuity with, and difference from Deuteronomy and, to some extent, other books of the Hebrew canon.

Deut 32 anticipates a resolution of the historical crisis, when God will have compassion on his servants and avenge the blood of his people. This resolution is described in TM 10 in the highly colorful language of theophany, but for the most part, the description of this theophany does not move beyond biblical descriptions of the Sinai occurrence or prophetic descriptions of an anticipated theophany (cf., e.g., Micah 1:1-4). Surely this is the language of myth, but this in itself is not sufficient to earn the unique label of "apocalyptic." More noteworthy is the manner in which our author transforms material regarding a past theophany from Mt. Sinai, found in Deut 33, into a picture of the future theophany. But even this Urzeit/Endzeit typology has its predecessors in, e.g., Isa 64:1ff., where the prophet longs for a theophany like that on Mt. Sinai. That God will appear soon "with fire" to judge decisively between his oppressed servants and their enemies is the contention of Third Isaiah (66:15f.). These chapters are well known for their promises of a new Jerusalem and the creation of a new heaven and a new earth. In all of this, setting and theological resolution, the similarities between TM and Third Isaiah are noteworthy, and attention should be drawn to the thesis of Paul D. Hanson that the roots of "apocalyptic" theology are, at least in part, to be found in Third Isaiah.[19]

An important point at which TM 10 diverges from its Deuteronomic prototype is in its contention that "the devil will be no more" (10:1). This statement regarding the obliteration of the cosmic force of evil carries with it a kind of finality which may well be moving beyond most of Hebrew eschatology. But even though the juxtaposition of this statement and the reference in v. 2 to the "ordaining" of Israel's patron angel appears to mirror a kind of ultimate ordeal between the principal celestial warriors,[20] this mythical dimension is more supposed than developed, and in this respect TM falls considerably short of the descriptions of celestial warfare in Dan 10.

Nevertheless, interest in the celestial realm appears at one other point: When God appears to punish the Gentiles, Israel will be exalted to the stars, and from that high vantage point, they will look down upon their enemies on the earth (10:9f.). In this bold image, we seem to have a complete and final separation of the heavenly and earthly realms, with the former becoming the dwelling of the righteous and the latter being transformed into the place of punishment. For this, there is no counterpart in Deuteronomy, and, indeed, the references to Satan and the great

---

[19] Paul D. Hanson, "Jewish Apocalyptic Against its Near Eastern Environment," RB 78 (1971), 49-54.

[20] Nickelsburg, Resurrection, pp. 28-31.

angel and to the exaltation of Israel appear to come from a tradition which is found also in Dan 13:1-3.[21]

The finality to which I have referred is evident at another point. Moses refers to the Lord's visitation in consummatione exitus dierum (1:18). In 12:4 this time is called exitus saeculi. The "discovery" of this book in the author's time indicates that the end, for which the present revelation is intended, is at hand. The idea and analogous terminology are familiar from Daniel.

But what of the relationship of this "revelation" to the ancient words of Moses? Harrington has spoken of partial and complete vindication. The words of Moses, uttered many centuries before, find their complete fulfilment in the coming theophany. For our author, the ancient prophecy was referring to his time, which is, by definition, the end of the age. Surely our author saw Moses' prophecy as being in some sense paradigmatic, but, more important, Moses was forecasting God's ultimate vindication of his people and the end of the present order, which is iminent. With reference to this finality, we are again in close theological proximity to the Book of Daniel.

This proximity appears at one other point, viz., TM's view of God's foreknowledge. It may be that the determinism in Daniel is partly a literary device born of the fact that a figure of the past is making an accurate forecast of events yet to come. It appears also to have parenetic value: hold fast, for at a stated time God will deliver his people. This latter function is also evident in TM 12. However, as Anitra Kolenkow has indicated, this determinism is also used in the service of an argument that God has intended the conviction of the Gentiles. This latter idea is in part allied to the biblical idea of God hardening the heart of the enemy king. It is apparent that with regard to TM and other similar books, we must be careful not to draw swift conclusions regarding the nature of the author's determinism. We need to study carefully the function of the teaching. One thing is clear: to whatever degree TM teaches a kind of determinism, this is in no way extended explicitly to all human actions, and the very use of the Deteronomic pattern implies clearly that people are responsible for their actions.

Our study of TM qua apocalyptic has been sketchy and only suggestive. Briefly stated, what appears to characterize our author's eschatology is its sense of finality, his consciousness that he lives at that time of the end of the age, toward which all history has been moving, and regarding which the prophet spoke of old. He envisions the destruction of the old order, the ultimate destruction of evil, and the final separation of the heavenly and terrestrial realms. In drawing his picture, he utilizes older mythical motifs and language. If we may venture a suggestion as to the difference of this eschatology from that, say, of Third Isaiah, it may lie in the explicitness with which he details the ultimacy of the judgment and its consequences, and the manner in which he splits the heavenly and earthly realms.[22] We have suggested some parallel phenomena in Daniel. However, the whole matter obviously needs much more discussion and study, and the appropriateness of the term "apocalyptic" is still open to question.

---

[21]Ibid., pp. 1-27,39-42.

[22]On this splitting of the two realms in apocalyptic, see Hanson, op. cit. (n. 19), pp. 35-58.

Finally, there is an interesting parallel between TM and the Qumran pešerim with respect to their understanding of revelation and inspiration. The commentaries evince the belief that the ancient prophets were speaking about the present time, which is understood to be the time of the end.[23] Moreover, the commentator on Habakkuk believes that God gave the Righteous Teacher unique insight to understand the mysteries of His servants the prophets (1QpHab 7:1-5), i.e., to understand that those mysteries referred to events of his own time. Without getting into the question of the cessation of prophecy, we may ask whether there is any substantive difference between the belief that the Teacher was inspired in his interpretation of the prophets, which interpretation embodied itself ultimately in commentaries, and our author's similar belief, which, however, led him to assume (or arrogate to himself) Moses' name and to rewrite prophecy? The difference in form is obvious. One maintains the integrity of the biblical text and comments on it. The other rewrites scripture. But is pseudonymous rewriting merely a literary device, or does it, in fact, witness to a self-understanding that is tantamount to a claim of prophecy that exceeds that of inspired interpretation of scripture? What is clear is that in both cases we have conclusions regarding the eschatological character of the present time tied to the understanding of canonical prophecy. The "mechanics" by which these conclusions were reached is a subject that might be considered. Perhaps we find a hint in Dan 9, if Daniel is, in fact, a cipher for the apocalyptist. The answer to Daniel's prayer is in the form of an angelophany in which Gabriel speaks in terms of the fulfilment of Jeremiah's prophecy regarding the restoration of Jerusalem.

Relationship to Parallel Traditions

The papers by Ralph Klein and Sheldon Isenberg indicate almost no relationship between TM and the peculiar textual traditions represented by the Greek Bible and the Targumim. In part, this conclusion must be viewed in light of the paucity of actual quotations of Deuteronomy in TM. There is a relatively small base on which to compare TM with the spectrum of text-critical evidence.

David Tiede discusses the portrait of Moses in TM and concludes that it is far more subdued in its praise of Moses than is the case in many contemporary writings.

By contrast, the Samaritan traditions evince many similarities with TM, as we have already noted. We may add only that form-critical analysis of the relevant portions of the Book of Joshua, set against the form-critical observations made above regarding TM and its putative narrative source may be helpful in an examination of the possible relationships between the two works and the typology of these relationships.

A final issue in connection with our construing of the topic of apocalyptic is raised by the tradition (attested in LAB and the midrash translated by Harold Attridge) that, before his death, Moses received a glimpse of heavenly things. Here we have the revelation not of events of the end time, but of heavenly things. As Michael Stone has noted in public lecture, this type of "apocalypse" has too often gone unobserved in discussions of revelatory literature.

George W.E. Nickelsburg, Jr.

---

[23] See Frank M. Cross, Jr., The Ancient Library of Qumran (Rev. ed.; Garden City, 1961), pp. 111-13.

THE DATE AND PROVENANCE OF THE TESTAMENT OF MOSES

John J. Collins

There is a wide variety of scholarly opinion on the date of the Testament of Moses.[1] We may distinguish three broad groups: those who believe TM was written about the time of the Maccabean revolt; those who assign a date in the first century A.D.; and those who date it after 70 A.D.[2]

I believe we can safely exclude the third of these possibilities. It is surely incredible that a work which is so largely a review of history could by-pass the fall of Jerusalem without reference.[3] Furthermore, at least two passages suggest that the temple was still standing when the book was written. In TM 8:9 we read that in the persecution preceding the final judgment the Jews will be forced to enter their "hidden place" --a probable reference to the holy of holies.[4] In TM 1:17-18 Joshua is told to hide this writing in earthen vessels "in the place He made from the beginning of the creation of the world that His name should be called upon until the day of repentance in the visitation wherewith the Lord shall visit them in the consummation of the end of the days."[5] This implies that the chosen

---

[1] I utilize the name, Testament of Moses, long agreed upon by scholars; cf. R.H. Charles, The Assumption of Moses (London, 1897), p.xlv.

[2] For a summary of early scholarship see Charles, Assumption, pp. xxi-xxviii. More recent scholarship is reviewed by E.-M. Laperrousaz, "Le Testament de Moïse," Semitica 19 (1970), pp. 88-99. The only important contribution which has appeared since the work of Laperrousaz is that of G.W.E. Nickelsburg Jr., Resurrection, Immortality, and Eternal Life in Intertestamental Judaism, HTS 26 (Cambridge, 1972), Excursus A, 43-45. Laperrousaz overlooks the important article of J. Licht, "Taxo, or the Apocalyptic Doctrine of Vengeance," JJSt 12 (1961), 95-103.

[3] The destruction of the temple in TM 6:9 is only partial. Most scholars recognise in this passage a reference not to the fall of the temple but the action of Sabinus, lieutenant of Varus in 4 B.C. Cf. Josephus Ant. 17.10,2,9,10 (254-64); 11,1 (295-98); JW 2.3,3 (49-50); 2.5,1-3 (66-79).

[4] "cogentur intrare in abditum locum eorum." Charles, Assumption, p. 32, suggests that this refers to the adyta of heathen temples which Jews were compelled to build under Antiochus Epiphanes (Josephus Ant.12.5,4 (253) cf. 1 Macc 1:47). It is difficult to see however how a temple or part thereof which the Jews themselves were building could be described as an "abditum locum."

[5] "in loco quem fecit ab initio creaturae orbis terrarum, ut invocetur nomen illius usque in diem paenitentiae in respectu quo respiciet illos Dominus in consummatione dierum." See Charles, Assumption, p. 8.

place remained the site for the invocation of God until the final judgment--therefore that the temple would not be destroyed. These considerations preclude definitively a date after the destruction of the temple.[6]

---

[6]Most scholars who argue for a later date identify the persecution described in ch 8 with the events immediately after the fall of Jerusalem (Rosenthal, Langen) or under Hadrian (Colani, Volkmar). See Charles, Assumption, pp. xxi-xxviii. We shall see that neither of these identifications is plausible. Two more recent attempts to date the book late must be considered.

Solomon Zeitlin, "The Assumption of Moses and the Revolt of Bar-Kokba," JQR 38 (1947), 1-45, asserts that a date before the destruction of the second Temple is out of the question and need not even be considered, because the method of designating an era by Anno Mundi was not used by Jews during the Second Commonwealth (cf. TM 1:2). This is not a reliable argument. In Jub 50:4, which is universally agreed to have been written in the period of the second Temple, the age of the world at the time of Moses is given as 2450 years. Now while the book of Jubilees is presented as a revelation to Moses of all the things that happened from the creation of the world to his time, TM is a revelation of the events from the time of Moses to the final judgment. Our manuscript of TM is part of a Latin manuscript which also contains the book of Jubilees. The date at the beginning of TM can then be most easily understood as an editorial attempt to put TM in sequence after Jubilees by dating it fifty years later (Jubilees is not dated to the death of Moses). Zeitlin's own dating of TM to 140 A.D. involves the supposition that the author wrote to predict a final judgment 350 years in the future (Zeitlin dates it to 490 A.D.). Taxo's statement to his seven sons that they should fast for three days meant that they should suffer for three hundred-year periods, and in the fourth hundred-year period go into the cave. These suppositions can only be dismissed as farfetched.

The recent attempt of Klaus Haacker, "Assumptio Mosis--eine samaritanische Schrift?" TZ 25 (1969), 385-405, to argue that TM was written by a Samaritan in the second century A.D. fails for lack of evidence. There is no reason why the place which God has chosen (TM 1:17) should refer to Gerizim rather than Jerusalem. (The association of Joshua with Shechem is not noted in TM.) The prominence of Moses is a trait common to several intertestamental works--notably Jubilees and the Qumran scrolls--and cannot be taken as an indication of Samaritan origin. The association of prophecy with Moses (TM 1:5; 3:11; 11:16) is based on Deut 18:15 and 34:10 and is also found in other apocalypses, e.g., 2 Bar 84. Finally, the division of 2 tribes and 10 tribes is adequately explained by the division of the 2 kingdoms. This is also paralleled in 2 Bar 1. Decisive against Haacker's theory is the lack of any clear reference to Samaria, Shechem, or Gerizim, while most of the book deals, undeniably, with Jewish history. His most specific argument on the date, viz., that crucifixion is not attested as a punishment for circumcision before the time of Hadrian, is debatable (cf. Josephus Ant. 12.5,4 [256]) and collapses in any case if we understand the passage as an eschatological tableau.

There are, then, two main possibilities for the date of TM.

1) A date in the period of Antiochus Epiphanes is supported by Licht and Nickelsburg. This period provides a very specific date for the work--after the outbreak of the persecution, but before the massacre of the Hasidim, described in 1 Macc 2:29-38 and 2 Macc 6:11.

2) The majority of scholars still support a date in the first century A.D. or around the turn of the era. Here the _terminus a quo_ is provided by the attack on the Jews under Varus, in 4 B.C., which seems to be referred to in TM 6:8-9.[7] Since Herod's children are said to reign for shorter periods than their father (who reigned for 34 years) and this was in fact true of only one of them (Archelaus), the _terminus ad quem_ is 30 A.D.--34 years after Herod's death. However, since the attack under Varus is the last explicit historical reference, the author probably wrote fairly soon thereafter.[8]

The point at issue between these conflicting interpretations is inextricably bound up with the literary-critical analysis of the book. If the book is a unity in its present form, it cannot be earlier than the death of Herod. However, some scholars have argued that there is more than one stratum in this book and that at least ch 6 is a later insertion.[9]

The Arguments Against the Unity of the Book

The case for regarding ch 6 as an interpolation and for dating the rest of the book in the time of Antiochus Epiphanes has most recently been expounded by George Nickelsburg.[10] There are four main arguments involved.

a) Nickelsburg has advanced a form-critical argument against the unity of the book. He argues that chs 5,8,9,10 constitute a pattern in which ch 6 has no place.

b) The similarity of the persecution in ch 8 to that which preceded the Maccabaean revolt.

c) The similarity of the figures of Taxo and his sons to the Hasidim who were killed at the outbreak of the Maccabaean revolt, and the literary affinities of the story of Taxo to other stories of Maccabaean times found in the books of Maccabees. Points (b) and (c) constitute the chief arguments for an early date.

d) The general affinity of the theology of the book to other works of the Maccabaean period.

---

[7]Josephus _Ant._ 17.10,2,9,10 (254-64); 11,1 (295-98); _JW_ 2.3,3 (49-50); 5,1-3 (66-79).

[8]TM 7:1 says that after this (the attack under Varus) the "four hours" will come. This is probably an apocalyptic formulation based on the "time, two times and half a time" of Dan 7:25. Cf. also Sib Or 5:155, where "after the fourth year a great star shines." In the present passage it may mean that TM was written less than four years after the attack under Varus.

[9]Cf. E. Stauffer, "Probleme der Priestertradition," _TLZ_ 81 (1956), col 141, describes TM as "ein ganzes Konglomerat von Vaticinien aus verschiedenen Epochen," of which the earliest date from the time of Antiochus, the latest from the time of Varus.

[10]Nickelsburg, _Resurrection_, pp. 43-45.

I suggest that none of these arguments is strong enough to warrant a division of the book, and that the evidence points rather to a date after the death of Herod for the whole book.

a) The form-critical argument

The form-critical argument advanced by Nickelsburg can carry no real weight. The pattern: (1) Sin; (2) Punishment; (3) Turning-point; (4) Salvation is certainly found in TM and, as Nickelsburg observes, has its roots in the latter part of Deuteronomy.[11] However, we are dealing with a pattern, not with a tightly knit literary form where the place of each element is strictly defined. So, in Nickelsburg's own paradigm, Deut 28-30, the pattern is interrupted by Deut 29, which does not fit under any of the four headings. We must be wary, then, of assuming that a passage has been inserted simply because it does not appear to contribute to a pattern. Besides, it is by no means clear why chapters 6 and 7 cannot be included under the heading sin. The exploits of the Hasmoneans and of Herod, as recounted here, could quite appropriately be classified under that heading.[12] There is then no form-critical reason to suppose that ch 6 has been inserted.

b) The similarity of TM 8 to the persecution of Antiochus

R.H. Charles was so impressed by the similarities between TM 8 and the accounts of the persection under Antiochus Epiphanes found in the books of Maccabees and Josephus that he suggested that chapters 8 and 9 originally stood after Ch 5 and before Ch 6 and so fitted into the chronological sequence of the book.[13] This suggestion has been decisively refuted by J. Licht.[14] The innocent death of Taxo in TM 9 brings about the divine vengeance in TM 10.[15] Accordingly, the logic of the apocalypse requires that TM 10 follow directly on TM 9. This conclusion allows two possible interpretations of TM 8-9. Either those chapters pro-

---

[11]Nickelsburg, Resurrection, p. 44, outlines the pattern as follows:

Sin	TM 5(also ch 2)	Deut 28:15
Punishment	8(also 3:1-4)	28:16-68
Turning-Point	9(also 3:5-4:4)	30:2
Salvation	10(also 4:5-9)	30:3-10

The parallelism here demonstrated between chs. 2-4 and chs. 5-10 strongly supports the basic analysis of the pattern.

[12]It is true that chs. 6 and 7 appear to recount what is at once punishment and sin, but this is in accordance with TM 5:1, which states the programme for the following chapters--"when the times of chastisement draw nigh and vengeance arises through the kings who share in their guilt and punish them."

[13]Charles, Assumption, pp. 28-30.

[14]Licht, "Taxo," pp. 95-103.

[15]M. Hengel, Die Zeloten (Leiden, 1961), p. 272. C. Lattey, "The Messianic Expectation in the Assumption of Moses," CBQ 4 (1942), 9-21, sees an intrinsic connection between chas. 8-9 and ch 10, because Antiochus is a type of Antichrist.

vide a historical account of the persecution of Antiochus Epiphanes[16] (in which case TM 6 must be regarded as an interpolation), or they constitute an eschatological tableau.[17]

The affinities of ch 8 to the persecution of Antiochus are obvious enough. They include the persecution of the Jews because of their circumcision, the medical disguise of circumcision, enforced idolatry and blasphemy. However, Laperrousaz points out that these affinities are not so complete as Charles had suggested.[18]

First, the assertion that Jews were crucified by Antiochus Epiphanes is found in no other Jewish writer before Josephus. Laperrousaz distorts his own point here when he claims that crucifixion was a specifically Roman form of punishment. In fact, it seems to have originated in the East, and could well have been used by Epiphanes.[19] However, it is remarkable that crucifixion is not mentioned in the books of Maccabees. It later became an extremely common form of punishment.[20] The narrative in Josephus which says that crucifixions took place under Antiochus Epiphanes is clearly more concerned with vividness than with historical accuracy.[21] At the time he wrote, Josephus might reasonably have presumed that crucifixion would have been used by Antiochus. The historicity of his account at this point must at least be suspect. There must accordingly be some doubt whether the reference to crucifixion in TM 8:1 can be a historical reference to the persecution of Antiochus.

---

[16]This is the position of Licht and Nickelsburg.

[17]This position has most recently been defended by Laperrousaz. See also Otto Eissfeldt, The Old Testament: An Introduction (New York, 1965), p. 624.

[18]Laperrousaz, Testament, pp. 122-24.

[19]Herodotus 1.128; 3.132 and 159; Thucydides 1.110,3. Herodotus uses the term $\dot{\alpha}\nu\alpha\sigma\kappa o\lambda\alpha\pi\acute{\iota}\zeta\epsilon\iota\nu$ and Thucydides $\dot{\alpha}\nu\alpha\sigma\tau\alpha\nu\rho o\tilde{\nu}\nu$ to refer to a method of execution by some form of crucifixion or impaling, used by the Persians. On its use by Greeks, Syrians and Romans, see K. Latte, "Todesstrafe," Pauly-Wissowa Real-Encyclopaedie, Supp. VII (1940), 1606, and W. Kasch, "$\Sigma\tau\alpha\upsilon\rho\acute{o}\varsigma$," TDNT 7 (1971), pp. 573-74.

[20]Cf. the mass crucifixions under Alexander Jannaeus, Josephus Ant. 13.14,2 (380) and JW 1.4,6 (97); 4QpNah 1:7-8. The Qumran text might be interpreted to mean that crucifixion has hitherto been unknown in Judaea: "and hangs men alive (a thing never done) formerly in Israel" (trans. G. Vermes, The Dead Sea Scrolls in English (Harmondsworth, 1962), p. 232.

[21]Josephus Ant. 12.5,4 (256): "And being on that account maltreated daily, and enduring bitter torments, they met their death. Indeed they were whipped, their bodies were mutilated, and while still alive and breathing they were crucified while their wives and the sons whom they had circumcised in despite of the king's wishes were strangled, the children being made to hang from the necks of their crucified parents . . . they too, poor wretches, wretchedly perished."

Second, TM says that even those who conceal their circumcision will be tortured.[22] This is nowhere recorded of the time of Antiochus Epiphanes.

Third, TM implies that the disguising of circumcision by medical operation would be a measure enforced against the will of the Jews. According to 1 Macc 1:16, this measure was deliberately undertaken by certain renegade Jews.

Fourth, the apparent use of "the Word" as a synonym for God is reminiscent of Targumic literature and might suggest a later date.

None of these points constitutes a decisive objection to seeing TM 8 as a historical account, but they show that the passage is not such a perfect replica of our other accounts of the time of Antiochus Epiphanes that it can be accepted as historical without further question. We must consider whether the passage cannot be more readily understood, with Laperrousaz, as an eschatological tableau.

The objection of Charles that eschatological woes could not be destribed as "a second visitation"[23] cannot be seriously maintained. Licht's article has shown that chs 8 and 9, whether historical or not, are "the final woes, precluding the theocratic kingdom."[24] The description "second" merely shows the parallelism with the first four chapters of the book which included reference to the Babylonian exile.

Nickelsburg attempts to dismiss the eschatological interpretation of the persecution as incompatible with the method of apocalyptic. He writes,

> The apocalyptic premise is that the author stands at the end of time. Immediately before his description of the judgment, he describes the events of his own time in great detail so that there may be no question as to when the judgment will come. As Moses is no exception. The author writes during Antiochus' persecution, which he elaborates in detail (chs 8-9), and there follows immediately a description of the judgment (ch 10).[25]

Nickelsburg offers no demonstration of the "apocalyptic premise." In fact, his statement is misleading. A more accurate generalization of apocalyptic patterns might say that the final judgment is preceded by a time of great distress, which may on occasion contain a historical description of the time of the author, but most often is future prediction, either entirely or in part.[26] Whether it contains historical material or not, this

---

[22] TM 8:2. Reading *celantes* (Charles) or *negantes* (Hilgenfeld). The text is corrupt and so this discrepancy with the persecution of Antiochus is doubtful.

[23] TM 8:1 (emendation of Schmidt-Merx); also TM 9:2.

[24] Charles, Assumption, p. 30. Cf. Licht, "Taxo," pp. 97f.

[25] Nickelsburg, Resurrection, p. 45, n. 14.

[26] See Lars Hartman, Prophecy Interpreted (Lund, 1966), p. 28:

> The texts to be considered often give the divine intervention a dark background, characterized by all kinds of evil, oppressions and irregularities. These descriptions of the background may include material from the author's own period,

time of distress is a stereotyped part of the apocalyptic pattern, characterized in later, Rabbinic literature as the "birth-pangs of the messiah." The time of woes is missing in only a few apocalypses--e.g., 1 Enoch 1-36 and 37-71 (Similitudes). It is a very regular feature of late first century A.D. apocalypses such as 4 Ezra and 2 Baruch,[27] but it also occurs in earlier apocalypses.[28] The apocalypse in which the eschatological woes most nearly coincide with the events of the author's time is the canonical book of Daniel. Yet even here there is an indication that there are some more woes to come.[29]

The patterns of apocalyptic thought provide no reason to assume that the final woes before the judgment describe historical events. They could possibly do so but in the majority of apocalypses they are stereotyped future predictions. Accordingly, if, as Nickelsburg assures us, TM "is no exception," we should probably interpret it as follows:

6:8-7:10: description of the author's own time
8:1-5: stereotyped description of the future eschatological woes.

The prediction in TM 8 is undeniably closely modelled on the persecution of Antiochus Epiphanes. This again conforms to the standard practice of apocalyptic writers. The eschatological events are patterned on events of the past. As another instance where the persecution under Antiochus provided the model for the eschatological woes we may point to Mark 13:14. Whether or not we regard this as an <u>ex eventu</u> prophecy, it is clear that the "abomination of desolation" is modelled on Dan 9:27. Again, the beast in Rev. 13 is clearly modelled on the representation of

---

for example the persecution of the faithful in TM 8:1ff. (!) and also motifs from the OT, for example, the family conflicts in Isa 19:2 or Mic 7:5f. The essential thing here is that this material has been, as it were, transposed and given a quite definite place in the historical scheme."

See also the treatment of the eschatological woes in Bousset-Gressmann, <u>Die Religion des Judentums</u> (Tübingen, 1926), p. 250 and P. Volz, <u>Die Eschatologie der jüdischen Gemeinde im neutestamentlicher Zeitalter</u> (Hildesheim, 1966), pp. 147-62; W. Bousset, <u>The Antichrist Legend</u> (London, 1896), pp. 218-231.

[27] E.g., 4 Ezra 6:9; 2 Bar 25; 32; 70.

[28] E.g., 1 Enoch 102; Jub 23; Sib Or 3:532-551; 796-807. In all the instances in this and the preceding note, woes are clearly future and of a mythical character. This is true even of Jub 23 which Nickelsburg, <u>Resurrection</u>, pp. 46f., also dates to the persecution of Antiochus Epiphanes - cf. Jub 23:25, "And the heads of the children shall be white with grey hair and a child of three weeks shall appear old like a man of hundred years."

[29] Cf. Dan 12:1: "At that time shall arise Michael, the great prince who has charge of your people. And there shall be a time of trouble such as there has never been since there was a nation till that time."

Antiochus Epiphanes in Dan 7.[30] If we understand TM 8 as an eschatological tableau, then the combination of precise parallels and minor discrepancies with the historical persecution becomes readily intelligible. The details of that persecution were available to the author from 1 and 2 Maccabees or from oral tradition. The detail of crucifixion was naturally prompted by the experience under Varus, referred to in TM 6:9. The disguising of circumcision would naturally appear as a punishment in the eyes of an apocalypticist portraying the final tableau.

Charles objected that it is incredible that the apocalypticist would have passed over the historical persecution under Antiochus, and the pollution of the temple without reference.[31] It is instructive to note that the events under Antiochus are passed over in silence in the cloud and waters vision in 2 Bar 66-67, although the author of that book was obviously interested in the temple. Besides, the author of TM had a special reason for by-passing this period. In ch 6 he reveals a bitter hatred for the Hasmonean house. Reference to the events in the time of Antiochus Epiphanes would have involved honouring the Maccabees, ancestors of the Hasmoneans.[32] The apocalypticist preferred to deny the events any significance. In fact it is possible, as we shall see, that he wanted to present Taxo as a countertype to the Maccabeans and so re-cast the Antiochan persecution in the future.

It is possible, as Nickelsburg suggests, that ch 5 refers to the Hellenizers before the Maccabean revolt, although the aptness of the reference to those who "are not priests, but slaves, sons of slaves," is more easily demonstrable with reference to John Hyrcanus.[33] A reference to the Hellenizers fits more easily in the historical sequence. It also means that TM is not without reference to the aspect of Antiochan times which it considered most significant.

c) Taxo

There is an extensive literature on the identification of Taxo.[34] No explanation of the name is fully satisfactory, but Rowley has adequately refuted all attempts to explain it by Gematria, and I accept Mowinckel's arguments that the word is derived from the Greek, τάξων, "orderer," probably reflecting an

---

[30] For the influence of the figure of Antiochus Epiphanes on the Jewish Antichrist legend see Bousset, Antichrist, pp. 158-170. See also B. Rigaux, L'Antechrist (Paris, 1932).

[31] Charles, Assumption, p. 29.

[32] The author could have referred to the events and reviled the Maccabees, but silence served his purpose just as well.

[33] Ant.13.10,5 (288-292) tells how at a banquet given by Hyrcanus a Pharisee requested that he lay down the high priesthood on the ground that his mother had been a captive.

[34] See H.H. Rowley, The Relevance of Apocalyptic (London, 1947), pp. 134-141; Laperrousaz, Testament, pp. 125-126; Nickelsburg, Resurrection, p. 97.

original Hebrew m^ehōqēq.[35] However, I find highly implausible Rowley's assertion that "the reference to his seven sons suggests that he was a real person, already existing, and not an ideal figure."[36] It is true that Taxo is not a messiah of a traditional type, but the stereotyped reference to seven sons and the generalized title "orderer" suggest that the author had an ideal figure in mind.[37]

Nickelsburg has drawn attention to the similarities between the story of Taxo in TM 9 and other stories from the Maccabean period. The other related stories are found in 1 and 2 Maccabees.

1 Macc 2:29-38 tells how a group of faithful Jews went down into the desert with their wives and children, were attacked on the sabbath, but chose to die rather than profane the sabbath by resisting. This group is usually identified with the Hasidim.[38] They died calling on heaven and earth to bear witness. This story is briefly recounted in 2 Macc 6:11.

1 Macc 2:15-28,49-64 recounts the story of Mattathias and his five sons, who also undertook to die in defence of the law. The element of passive resistance is missing in this case.

In 2 Macc 7 we read of the martyrdom of a mother and seven sons for their fidelity to the law. Here again the details are different. The brothers have been arrested, so that we do not

---

[35] S. Mowinckel, "The Hebrew Equivalent of Taxo in Ass. Mos. ix," SVT 1 (Leiden, 1953), pp. 78-87. Mowinckel, He That Cometh (New York, 1955), pp. 300f. Mowinckel's suggestion is supported by M. Delcor, RB 62 (1955), 60-75; F.M. Cross, The Ancient Library of Qumran (Rev. ed.; New York, 1961), p. 228, n. 73; and Nickelsburg, Resurrection, p. 98, n. 33.

[36] Rowley, Apocalyptic, p. 137.

[37] Cf. Mowinckel, "The Hebrew Equivalent," p. 89:
In the structure of the book Taxo belongs to the future, but it may very well be assumed that some historical person of the time of the author, or a somewhat earlier time, has served as a model to this figure.
The use of the future participle τάξων is probably meant to underline the fact that Taxo is a future figure.
J. Jeremias, "Ἠλίας", TDNT 2 (1964), p. 933, has suggested that the name "orderer" indicates affinity of the figure of Taxo with the second coming of Elijah.

[38] The Hasidim are mentioned explicitly in 1 Macc 2:42, where they are said to join Mattathias after he had resolved to fight on the sabbath if necessary. They are described as an "assembly" (συναγωγή) and "everyone who offers himself freely." In 1 Macc 7:9 they are mentioned in connection with some scribes who negotiated with Alcimus. In 2 Macc 14:6, Alcimus accuses the Hasidim as the followers of Judas Maccabaeus. Various attempts have been made to reconstruct the nature and ideology of this party. See especially V. Tcherikover, Hellenistic Civilization and the Jews (Philadelphia, 1959), pp. 125f., and M. Hengel, Judentum und Hellenismus, WUNT 10 (Tübingen, 1969), pp. 319-29.

know whether they offered any resistance.[39]

There are undoubted similarities between those stories and the story of Taxo. The question of priority and of the direction of the influence remains to be solved.

In the belief that he has already established the date of TM, Nickelsburg assumes that "behind all these variants was a story about a prominent Hasid and his seven sons"--the story of Taxo. Since we do not accept that the date of TM has yet been established, we must proceed more cautiously.

There are two elements in the stories which are undoubtedly historically accurate for the time of Antiochus Epiphanes. One is the fact that Mattathias and his five sons led a revolt against the king. The other is the fact that a group of faithful Jews, to whom we refer as Hasidim were massacred in a cave on a sabbath. In the case of Mattathias, there is no reason to doubt that he exhorted his sons to die in defence of the law and reminded them of the achievements of their ancestors. Both of those features are also found in the story of Taxo. If we are to assume that either story has been influenced by the other, it is surely easier to assume the priority of the story of Mattathias, who we know existed historically, than of that of Taxo, who is in doubt.[40]

They story of the mother and seven sons in 2 Macc 7 carries less historical probability than the other stories. It may reflect some actual event in the course of the persecution, but the idea of a mother with seven sons is so stereotyped that it must be suspect.[41] In fact this story has all the hallmarks of a paradigmatic invention--a typical, ideal, example of the kind of thing that happened under Antiochus Epiphanes.[42] The points of contact with the story of Taxo are slight--the number seven, the resolve to die rather than transgress the law, and the appeal to God for vengeance. Now the number seven is equally suspect in both cases because of its widespread use as an ideal number. The resolve to die rather than transgress the law was obviously widespread at the time of the Maccabean revolt, but also recurs again and again in later Jewish history--notably on the lips of the Zealots.[43] The appeal for vengeance is rooted in the OT and also

---

[39]Charles, Assumption, p. 33, argues that the story of Eleazar in 2 Macc 6 is also related. Charles would argue that TM derived the figure of the parent from Eleazar. Nickelsburg sees the story of Taxo as original and thinks that 2 Macc 6 and 2 Macc 7 preserved different elements, Resurrection, p. 101.

[40]The details which roughly correspond in the two stories are listed by Nickelsburg, Resurrection, p. 100.

[41]Cf. Jer 15:9; 1 Sam 1:5; Job 42:13.

[42]The abbreviator of the history of Jason of Cyrene was interested in presenting this type of generalized example rather than in historical detail. Cf. 2 Macc 2:19-31.

[43]See M. Hengel, Die Zeloten, pp. 261-76 (Die Bereitschaft zum Martyrium).

recurs later than the Maccabean revolt.[44] Accordingly, there is no need to assume that either 2 Macc 7 or TM 9 is historical because they have these motifs in common. The two stories could have developed independently. The story in 2 Macc has no reference to a cave and lacks the specifically pacifistic stance of the story of Taxo.

Even if we assume interdependence between the story of Taxo and 1 and 2 Maccabees, it is unlikely that the Taxo story is the earlier. TM 9 combines elements from each of the other stories. The father with several sons resembles Mattathias. The specific number seven recalls the mother and her sons in 2 Macc 7. The setting in the cave and the pacifistic ethic resembles the story of the Hasidim in 1 Macc 2. It is easier to assume that the author of TM combined these various elements into one story, rather than to suppose that the Taxo story was original and that each of the other stories borrowed different elements from it.

The most striking argument for an early date for TM is its similarity to the story of the Hasidim who were massacred on the sabbath. The points of correspondence include the setting in the cave, the deliberate resolution to die rather than transgress the law, and the appeal to God for vengeance.

However, these points of contact are of quite a general nature and lack the specificity which would allow an identification. This is true even of the setting in the cave. Throughout the intertestamental period, Jews sought refuge in caves in the wilderness in time of distress.[45] A number of such cases are recorded during the reign of Herod. One of them shows remarkable similarity to the Taxo story. It tells of a man who killed himself, his wife and his seven sons rather than submit to Herod.[46] Accordingly, we must accept that the cave setting was a standard feature of Jewish revolts and refugees at any time from the Maccabees to the war with Rome.

The form of pacifism in the two stories shows striking, but not perfect resemblance. The Hasidim in 1 Macc fail to resist because of the sabbath, but are later characterised as valiant warriors.[47] TM gives the impression of general pacifism, although the three day fast may indicate that they were going into the cave to celebrate a festival.[48] TM 9 cannot refer to precisely the same incident as 1 Macc 2, although it reflects a similar attitude. The question is, whether the pacifistic attitude of the Hasidim recurs at later times, and whether the attitude of

---

[44]As Nickelsburg has noted, Resurrection, p. 97, the obvious source of this motif in TM is Deut 32:43. For later examples of this, see 1 Enoch 47:1-4; Rev 6:9.

[45]See especially Hengel, Zeloten, pp. 255-61.

[46]Ant. 14.15,5 (429-30).

[47]1 Macc 2:42.

[48]Cf. A. Jaubert, La Notion d'Alliance dans le Judaisme, Patristica Sorbonensia 6 (Paris, 1963), p. 259. Jaubert refers to 1QSa 1:26, which requires a three day period of sanctification before a solemn feast, and 2 Macc 10:6, which mentions how some Jews spent the feast of Tabernacles in caves. Jaubert suggests the Passover or Tabernacles.

Taxo could plausibly reflect the attitude of a group of Jews around the turn of the era?

I believe this question must be answered in the affirmative. Passive resistance remained a live option throughout the intertestamental period, even though it was usually overshadowed by militancy. We have at least one instance where it was successfully applied in practice. When Pilate threatened to slaughter a crowd of Jews at Caesarea, when they gathered to protest against the Roman standards in Jerusalem, they lay on the ground and bared their necks for the sword rather than break their law. Pilate had the standards removed.[49] Non-retaliation and passive resistance are advocated in a number of intertestamental writings --notably the Qumran scrolls and the NT.[50] It should be noted, too, that the motif of divine vengeance plays a prominent part in those later texts. So the Qumran community undertook not to "return evil to anybody" and not to undertake "the trial of a man of perdition until the Day of Vengeance,"[51] and Paul exhorted the Romans,

> Beloved do not avenge yourselves but give room for the Wrath; for it is written, 'To me belongs vengeance, I will repay" says the Lord. Rather, if your enemy is hungry, give him to eat, if he is thirsty, give him to drink. For in so doing you will heap coals of fire on his head.[52]

It appears, then, that the persecution of Antiochus is not the only possible milieu in which TM 9 could have been written. An equally plausible provenance can be suggested at any time in the centuries immediately before and after the turn of the era.

d) **The affinities of TM with other documents of the 2nd century**

While TM cannot be shown to be a source for the books of Maccabees, the question may yet be raised whether its affinities with the literature of the second century B.C. require an early dating for TM. In addition to the parallels with 1 and 2 Maccabees, Nickelsburg has drawn attention to similarities between the

---

[49] JW 2.9,1-3 (169-74). Cf. also the confrontation between Petronius and the Jews when Caligula wanted to place a statue in the Jerusalem temple (JW 2.10,4 (195-98); Ant. 18.8,3 (269-72).

[50] See G.W. Buchanan, *The Consequences of the Covenant*, SNT 20 (Leiden, 1970), pp. 31-41; K. Stendahl, "Hate, Non-Retaliation and Love," HTR 55 (1962), 343-56.
It should be noted that the Jews refrained from war on the sabbath on several occasions later than the Maccabean revolt, notably during the campaign of Pompey, JW 1.7,3 (146); Ant. 14.4, 2 (63); cf. JW 2.16,4 (392). Also the sabbatical years were observed: 1 Macc 6:49 explains the fall of Bethsura as due to the "sabbath to the land." JW 1.2,4 (60) and Ant. 13.8,1 (234) record that Hyrcanus abandoned the siege of Dagon because of the sabbatical year. See R. North, "The Maccabean Sabbatical Years," Biblica 34 (1953), 501ff.; Y. Yadin, *The Scroll of the War of the Sons of Light against the Sons of Darkness*, (Oxford, 1962), pp. 5 and 20, n. 1.

[51] 1QS 10:17-20.

[52] Rom 12:17-21, trans. Stendahl, "Hate, Non-Retaliation, and Love," p. 345.

judgment scene in TM 10 and Dan 12 and other early apocalypses.[53] However, since Nickelsburg himself finds the same pattern of judgment scene in such late apocalypses as 4 Ezra and 2 Baruch and Revelation, we can draw no conclusions as to the date on this basis.[54]

The relation of TM to the book of Daniel is far from clear. In TM 4:1 we read of a leader of the Jews during the exile who makes intercession for them. Most scholars have seen here a reference to Dan 9:4-19.[55] If this is correct, the author of TM must have known of the tradition that Daniel prayed for the Jews. This is most easily explained by assuming that he knew the book of Daniel, and therefore wrote at a later point. However, he could conceivably have known an independent tradition about Daniel--perhaps the tradition used by the author of the canonical book. So this point is indecisive.

More important are a number of parallels between TM and later apocalypses, such as 2 Baruch and 4 Ezra, on points which are not attested in the 2nd century B.C. apocalypses such as Daniel, Jubilees, or the earlier parts of Enoch. Among these parallels we may note two in particular.

The idea that God created the world on behalf of his people is not formulated in any work before the turn of the era but occurs very frequently in the late first century A.D.[56]

There is much importance attached to the role of a human mediator between God and man in TM. Now the idea of mediation is certainly old in Israel, but in the apocalyptic literature of the early second century B.C., the role of mediator is usually given to an angelic figure,[57] whereas human intercession attains a much more prominent role in the apocalypses of the late first century A.D. In particular the words of Joshua to Moses in TM 11

---

[53]Chiefly Jub 23 and Test. Judah 20:25, Nickelsburg, Resurrection, pp. 28-42.

[54]The use of language from Second and Third Isaiah mentioned by Nickelsburg, Resurrection, p. 44, n. 14, as a possible indication of an early date is also indecisive as the language of these books was still used, e.g., by NT authors. The role of the angel in TM 10 finds its closest parallels in 1QM, 11Q Melch and Rev 12. The figure was obviously current throughout the intertestamental period. The elevation of Israel to the stars in TM 10 has no precise parallel anywhere, but the assimilation of the just to the stars after death is found in a wide range of apocalypses from Dan 12:3 to 2 Bar 51:10.

[55]Charles, Assumption, p. 14, Laperrousaz, Testament, p. 117. Ezra might also be considered, but this would involve an obvious anachronism.

[56]TM 1:12; 4 Ezra 6:55,59; 7:11; cf. 2 Bar 14:18,19; 15:7; 21:24 etc.

[57]Cf. Dan 12:1; 1 Enoch 90:17,22; 104:1; Test. Judah 20:5, Nickelsburg, Resurrection, pp. 12-14.

[58]Dan 9 provides one possible instance, but nothing is said to suggest that Daniel here is a father figure with an established role of intercessor. Cf. Moses in TM 11:9-19.

recall 2 Bar 32:9, where the people lament at the departure of Baruch,

> Whither departest thou from us, Baruch, and forsakest us as a father who forsakes his orphan children?[59]

These parallels suggest that TM may be nearer in time to 2 Baruch than to Daniel or the earlier parts of Enoch.[60]

Some explanation may be sought for the many parallels between TM and the stories from Maccabean times which evidently provide many of the motifs for chs 8 and 9. We have already seen that TM is bitterly opposed to the Hasmonean house.[61] I venture to suggest that Taxo is proposed as an antitype to Mattathias, father of the Maccabees.

There are several parallels and some sharp contrasts between Mattathias and Taxo:

M. is of an obscure priestly family. T. is "a man of the tribe of Levi."[62]

M. has five sons. T. has the perfect number, seven.

Both perform ascetic rites: M. and his sons rend their clothes. T. and his sons fast.

Both note the impiety of the nations.[63]

M. flees to the hills, T. to a cave.

Both exhort their sons to die for the law. In M's case, this means active resistance, in T's case, passive.

Both appeal to the example of the fathers.

Both find their strength in the law.

M. looks to Judas for vengeance. T. looks to God.

So amid the extensive parallels we find a number of pointed contrasts--the priestly credentials, the number of sons, the manner of resistance, the source of vengeance. In each case Taxo appears the more pious and perfect Jew.

The significance that such an antitype of Mattathias might have had around the turn of the era becomes clear if we bear in

---

[59] Cf. also 2 Bar 2:1-2, where God says that Jerusalem cannot be taken while Jeremiah is in it.

[60] Among the other parallels between TM and 2 Baruch we may mention the distinction within Israel of 10 tribes and 2 tribes-- TM 2:3,5; 3:4, etc.; 2 Bar 1:3-- and the role of Moses as prophet of future things in TM 1:15 and in 2 Bar 84:5. Of course both of these points could be derived independently from the OT. TM was grouped with 2 Baruch and 4 Ezra by F. Rosenthal, Vier Apokryphischen Bücher aus der Zeit und Schule R. Akibas (Leipzig, 1885).

[61] TM 6:1.

[62] The priesthood of the Hasmoneans is assailed in TM 6:1.

[63] Note however the affinity of TM 9:3 with 4 Ezra 3:29,31: "Are their deeds any better that inhabit Babylon." The reference in 1 Macc 2:10 lacks the complaint about the relative merits and sufferings of the nations.

mind the role played by the memory of the Maccabees in the popular nationalist ideology.[64] The festivals of Hanukkah and Nicanor's Day kept the memory of the Maccabees alive.[65] Josephus records the popular enthusiasm which greeted the emergence of descendents of the Hasmoneans in the days of Herod and after Herod's death.[66] Particularly interesting in this respect is the popular reception of the imposter who claimed to be Herod's son Alexander, descended from the Hasmoneans through his mother, Mariamne. He emerged on the scene shortly after Varus had surpressed the revolt in Jerusalem in 4 B.C., and he won wide support from Jews in Crete, Melos, and Rome. He claimed to be concerned that the posterity of Mariamne might not be completely wiped out.[67] This imposter must be seen in the context of a line of messianic pretenders who led abortive movements in the first century.[68] From this it appears that Hasmonean descent could be a factor of real importance in the nationalist movement at the turn of the era. Even when there was no claim of descent from the Hasmoneans, the influence of the Maccabees on nationalist ideology appears in the recurrence of Maccabean names among the leaders of the Zealots.[69]

While Maccabean influence was only one factor among many in the development of Jewish nationalism,[70] it was a real factor, especially around the turn of the era when descendents of the Hasmonean house were still available. Wherever Maccabean motifs are found in Jewish nationalism, they are always associated with

---

[64]See especially W.R. Farmer, Maccabees, Zealots, and Josephus (New York, 1956), pp. 125-58. See also the review of M. Avi-Yonah, IEJ 8 (1958), 202-204, and the comments of Hengel, Zeloten, 176-78. Avi-Yonah and Hengel note the differences between the Maccabees and the Zealots, particularly the fact that the Maccabees arose in a time of religious persecution, whereas the Zealots were primarily nationalists. They do not, however, shake Farmer's argument that the Zealots saw themselves as followers of the Maccabees.

[65]Farmer, Maccabees, pp. 132-51. The recollection of a number of Maccabean victories is preserved in the Megillath Taanith, from the late first century A.D.

[66]When Aristobulus, grandson of Aristobulus II, was proclaimed high priest by Herod, "there arose among the people an impulsive feeling of affection toward him and there came to them a vivid memory of the deeds performed by his grandfather Aristobulus. Being overcome, they gradually revealed their feelings ..." (Ant. 15.3,3 (51-52). The display of popular emotion aroused Herod's jealousy, and he had the youth murdered.

[67]Ant. 17.12,1 (324-38).

[68]See Hengel, Zeloten, pp. 235-38, 296-307. Alexander did not claim to be a messiah in the eschatological sense, but he claimed to be rightful king of the Jews, and he resembled the other pretenders in attempting to lead a revolt.

[69]See W.R. Farmer, "Judas, Simon and Athronges," NTS 4 (1958) 147-55. Cf. also the persistence of the motif of "zeal" in both movements.

[70]It has probably been exaggerated by Farmer, but it was nevertheless a real and considerable factor.

violent rebellion. If TM wished to present Taxo as an antitype of Mattathias, it was making a statement against the popular ideology of violent revolution which had been pioneered by Mattathias and which was to bring disaster on Judaism in the first century A.D. Against this ideology it set the model of pacifistic piety which relied on the perfect observance of the law and was content to wait for the vengeance of God. This piety had its model in the Hasidim of Maccabean times but also had some adherents throughout the intertestamental period.

I conclude, then, that we have no adequate reason to deny the unity of TM. The book can be dated by its latest historical reference to a time shortly after the campaign of Varus in 4 B.C.

Provenance

The exact provenance of the book is more problematic. At one time or other, its author has been assigned to every known Jewish sect of the period.[71] Some of these suggestions can be easily discounted. The pacifistic stance of the book is directly at variance with the policy of the Zealots, and the eschatological orientation excludes a Sadducean origin.[72] Since Charles, a number of scholars have argued that the book was written by a Pharisaic quietist.[73] Charles, however, arrived at this conclusion by a process of elimination. There is nothing in the book to tie it specifically to Pharisaism.[74] Against this hypothesis, Pharisaism seems to have expected a traditional messiah, rather than intervention by an angel, or directly by God, as envisaged in TM 10.[75]

A number of parallels can be found between TM and the Qumran writings.[76] These parallels include the hatred of the Hasmonean

---

[71] Including the Samaritans (above n. 6). See the review by Laperrousaz, Testament, pp. 88-95.

[72] Cf. also a possible attack on the Sadducees in TM 7. On the Sadducees, see the recent work of J. le Moyne, Les Sadducéens (Études bibliques; Paris, 1972).

[73] Charles, Assumption, pp. li-liv. Most recently Charles has been followed by G. Reene, Die Geschichte Israels in der Auffassung des frühen Judentums (Diss. Heidelberg, 1967). I have not seen this work.

[74] For our criteria in determining whether a pre-Rabbinic document is Pharisaic, we are largely dependent on Josephus, JW 2.8,14 (162-63); Ant. 18.1,3 (12-15); 13.5,9 (172). In TM there is no belief in resurrection, no discussion of fate or free will. A belief in angels is attested in TM 10, but this belief was shared by other Jews, such as those of Qumran.

[75] Admittedly we know little of early Pharisaism. If the Pss of Solomon can be taken as evidence, Pharisees of the first century B.C. expected a Davidic messiah.

[76] An Essene origin was originally suggested by M. Schmidt-A. Merx, "Die Assumptio Mosis mit Einleitung und erklärenden Anmerkungen," in Adelbert Merx, Archiv für wissenschaftliche Erforschung des Alten Testaments 1 (Halle, 1868), pp. 111-52. Recently it has been endorsed by A. Dupont-Sommer, Aperçus préliminaires sur les Manuscripts de la Mer Morte (Paris, 1950), p. 115, M. Delcor, "Contribution," p. 60, and Laperrousaz. Mowinckel,

house,[77] the general priestly interest of TM,[78] the emphasis on the covenant,[79] the role of the angel contrasted with Satan in TM 10,[80] the deferment of resistance in expectation of divine vengeance,[81] possibly also the name Taxo.[82] It is also possible that TM 7 is an attack on the Pharisees,[82] and this too can be paralleled from the Qumran sect.

However, there are also objections which must be made against ascribing this document to the Qumran sect. First, it contains no reference to an organized community. Second, no fragments of the work have been found at Qumran. It is possible, of course, that such fragments may yet be found, but in view of the abundance of material we now have from Qumran, I believe that the absence of TM must for the present be accepted as decisive.[83]

The fact that TM is not attested at Qumran is also a considerable argument against the hypothesis that Taxo was a historical leader of the Hasidim in Maccabean times. If Taxo was the spiritual ancestor of the Qumran community, could it be possible that a work which was a virtual last will and testament of him and his group could be neglected by that community, while the story influenced the history of the Maccabees and Hasmoneans, the archrivals of the Qumran sect?[84]

The fact remains that TM is a sectarian document. This is most clearly shown by their rejection of the worship of the Second Temple. TM 4:8 alleges that at the time of the return from the exile "the two tribes will continue . . . sad and lamenting because they will not be able to offer sacrifices to the Lord of

---

"The Hebrew Equivalent," and Jaubert, La Notion d'Alliance, p. 260, also incline to this view.

[77] TM 6:1. Cf. especially H.J. Schoeps, "Die Opposition gegen die Hasmonäer (Der gegenwärtige Stand der Erforschung der in Palastina neu gefundenen Handschriften)," TLZ 81 (1956), 663-670; Cross, Ancient Library, pp. 127-60.

[78] Cf. the frequent references to temple and sacrifice, TM 2:4,6,8,9; 3:2; 4:8; 5:3f.; 6:1-9.

[79] This is especially emphasized by Jaubert, La Notion d'Alliance, p. 260.

[80] Cf. Nickelsburg, Resurrection, pp. 39-40.

[81] Cf. Stendahl, "Hate, Non-Retaliation, and Love."

[82] TM 7:3-10. Cf. Matt 23:5,6,25; Mark 12:40. Jaubert, La Notion d'Alliance, pp. 259f.

[83] The Essenes were also thought to be friendly to Herod, Ant. 15.10,4-5 (371-378). It is possible that some Essenes shared the widespread hatred of that king, but the strong antipathy to Herod in TM 6 must strengthen our doubts about the Essene authorship of the book.

[84] This anomalous conclusion follows if we accept Nickelsburg's dating of TM and his theory that TM influenced 1 and 2 Maccabees.

their fathers.[85] Other vaguer points also betray this sectarian consciousness: Israel will be divided as to the truth (5:1) and Taxo's forefathers did not tempt God so as to transgress his commands.[86]

We can say, then, that TM was produced by a sectarian group around the turn of the era. This group was marked by antagonism to Herod and the Hasmoneans and the rejection of the contemporary temple cult. It called for a complete return to the Mosaic law. Its model of complete observance involved the sharp rejection of militant nationalism, whether in the Hasmonean or Zealot traditions. It shows certain parallels with the Qumran writings. These parallels suggest that the book may have been written by a group of Essenes, or a group close to the ideology of the Essenes. However, in view of the lack of any indication of an organized community, and above all the absence of the document from the finds at Qumran, it is unlikely that TM was written or preserved in the Qumran community.

---

[85] This rejection of the worship of the entire Second Temple is conceivable in the case of a first century Essene, after the party had been excluded from the temple for nearly 200 years, but not in the case of "the priestly wing of the Hasidic movement" (Nickelsburg, Resurrection, p. 45), the Zadokite clergy who controlled the temple before their departure to Qumran.

[86] TM 9:4. Contrast the denunciation of the sins of Israel in the earlier chapters. Cf. Mowinckel, "The Hebrew Equivalent," p. 95. The attack on religious exclusivism in TM is ironic in a sectarian document, but the sectarian mind is usually insensitive to irony.

John J. Collins
Saint Mary of the Lake Seminary
Mundelein, Illinois

AN ANTIOCHAN DATE FOR THE TESTAMENT OF MOSES

George W.E. Nickelsburg, Jr.

In the previous paper, John Collins has offered a thorough and systematic critique of the early dating of TM proposed by Licht and further argued by myself. In this brief paper, I shall speak to the issues that Collins has raised and shall attempt in general to sharpen my own arguments.

As Collins indicates, the two feasible alternatives for dating TM are (1) during Antiochus' persecution and (2) during the reign of the Herods. Licht's analysis has shown that it is impossible to interpose chs 6-7 between chs 9 and 10, as Charles suggested. Thus if we accept chs 6-7 as original to the composition, we must read chs 8-9 as a prediction of future events cast in the mold of events from the Antiochan persecution. This alternative is the position of Collins, as well as Günther Reese and E.-M. Laperrousaz.[1] We turn now to Collins' examination of my arguments.

a) The form-critical argument

Collins is surely correct that we need not look for a slavish imitation of the scheme of Deuteronomy. In fact, my schematization of TM 2-10 should be modified as follows:

1. Sin	TM 5-6:1	(TM 2)	Deut 28:15	
a. Punishment	6:2-9			
b. Sin	7			
2. Punishment	8	(3:1-4)	28:16-68	
3. Turning Point[2]	9	(3:5-4:4)	30:2	
4. Salvation	10	(4:5-9)	30:3-10	

This, in turn, raises a difficulty for the later dating. If ch 5 refers to the Hellenizers, as seems certain,[3] we have no reference to a specific punishment for the Hellenizers. Rather, the deeds of Herod and Varus are described as the punishment of both the Hellenizers and the Hasmonaeans. This problem is solved if we count chs 6-7 as an interpolation: ch 8 is a description of Antiochus, bringing judgment on the Hellenizers,[4] and the group-

---

[1]Günther Reese, Die Geschichte Israels in der Auffassung des frühen Judentums (Diss. Heidelberg, 1967), pp. 104f.; E.-M. Laperrousaz, Le Testament de Moïse, Semitica 19 (1970), p. 122.

[2]Daniel Harrington correctly notes that the Taxo story does not represent the kind of repentance envisioned in Deut 30 (see below, pp. 65f.). Nevertheless, Taxo's death is a deliberate human act calculated to force divine vengeance. For this there is no counterpart in Deut 32. It appears then to represent (in our author's view) the appropriate counterpart to the element of repentance.

[3]Collins grants this. On the problems, see Nickelsburg, Resurrection, Immortality, and Eternal Life In Intertestamental Judaism, HTS 26 (Cambridge, 1972), pp. 44f.

[4]Jonathan Goldstein suggests in a subsequent paper that ch 6 preserves references to Antiochus from the earlier form of the document. This theory, as I understand it, means that Antiochus

ing together of the Hellenizers and the Hasmonaeans is a literary accident.[5]

b) The similarity of TM 8 to the persecution of Antiochus

As Collins himself notes, none of his arguments regarding the dissimilarities between TM 8 and other accounts of Antiochus' persecution are decisive. Most important, and indeed decisive, for his argument is Collins' claim regarding the nature of apocalyptic descriptions of the end-time. My contention, as quoted by Collins, is that in the literary genre of apocalypses, i.e., more or less detailed descriptions of the events leading up to and comprising the end-time, the events contemporary to the author are described in increased and explicit detail, so as to make their identity unmistakable. Examples of this are Dan 7, Dan 11, Jub 23:14-23, and perhaps En 89-90. I include the material in TM 8-9 in this category.

According to Collins, however, it is "a more accurate generalization of apocalyptic patterns . . . that the final judgment is preceded by a time of great distress, which may on occasion contain a historical description of the time of the author, but most often is future prediction, either entirely or in part." He then offers this outline:

TM 6:8-7:10   Description of the author's own time
   8:1-5   Stereotyped description of the future eschatological woes

Thus he sees ch 8 as part of an eschatological tableau.

But are the events of TM 8:1-5 stereotyped and analogous to other future predictions? The parallel passages cited by Collins do not, I suggest, bear out the comparison. These predictions of future woes include materials of two types.

Mythical descriptions of (celestial) judgment and cosmic cataclysm (En 102:1-3; Sib Or 3:538-44, 796-807; 4 Ezra 6:21-24)[6]

Generalized descriptions of human strife, wars, woes, and upheavals (Sib Or 3:533-36; 4 Ezra 9:3; 2 Bar 25; 70)

Over against these, TM 8:1-5 is quite specific and unique: crucifixion of those who confess circumcision; wives being given to the gods; sons being operated on; the pious being forced to bear pagan idols, to enter "their inmost sanctuary," and to blaspheme.

Collins cites Mark 13:14 and Rev 13 as examples where the persecution under Antiochus and Antiochus himself provide the models for descriptions of future woes. However, in the case of Mark, there is no evidence that the evangelist is aware that Dan

---

is introduced into the narrative with considerable description on two separate occasions in close proximity to one another--which, of course, is not fatal to the theory. His reconstruction makes the earlier date easier to accept and perhaps more plausible. However, I have argued independently of his reconstruction.

[5] It is no accident that the redactor puts the Hellenizers and Hasmonaeans in the same category. It is, however, a literary accident that the sins of both are seen as punished by the acts of Herod and Varus.

[6] Similarly, as Collins notes (n. 28), Jub 23:15 involves a kind of mythical description.

9:27 referred to the Antiochan persecution. He appears, rather, to be citing the fulfilment of a Danielic prophecy. Moreover, the expression "abomination of desolation" is quite vague and is different in kind from the events described in TM 8. Similarly, the seer in Rev 13 shows no awareness of the original historical referent of the beast in Dan 7, but seems, rather, to be reusing an apocalyptic tradition with heavy mythical overtones. In short I do not find that the parallels cited by Collins support his contention that we are dealing here with a common device of prediction based on a type in the past.

It is, of course, a moot question, whether any given apocalyptist could or would exclude reference to Antiochus' persecution. In the present case, however, such an exclusion cannot be explained, as Collins does, by the author's antipathy toward the Hasmonaean house. Dan 11, to cite one example, makes only passing, indeed pejorative, reference to the Hasmonaeans. Especially if one wishes to press the pacifist tendencies in TM, one would not expect that any reference to the persecution would mention the Hasmonaeans' battles. What is curious, if we accept the later date, is this aggregation of facts: the deletion of all reference to the persecution as punishment; the description of the acts of Herod and Varus as such punishment; and then the use of the persecution material as a typological description of future woes.

It is clear that in its present form, which dates from Herodian times, TM does use a description of events from the time of Antiochus as part of a kind of eschatological tableau. We may suppose that the author/redactor got his description from a source. In view of the considerations above, it seems best to identify that source as an earlier form of TM itself.

c) Taxo

I have noted the following similarities among the stories in question.[7]

	1 Macc 2: 29-38	TM 9	1 Macc 2 15-28, 49ff.	2 Macc 7
Antiochan times	x	x	x	x
Set in a cave	31	6	-	-
Parent	(30,38)	Father	Father	Mother
and sons		7 sons	sons	7 sons
Decree "enforced"	-	-	15	1
Command to obey	33	-	18	(7)
Promise of riches	-	-	18	24
Refusal	34	-	22	30
Let us die	37	6	50	2,29
(rather than transgress)	-	6	-	2,29
Appeal to God/	37	7	67	37f.
or vengeance				8:3
Mourning		6	14	
Contrast of Israel & nations		3	19f.	
Retreat		6	28f.	
Evil times		2	49	
Example of fathers		4	51-61	
Strength in Torah		5	64	

---

[7] Nickelsburg, Resurrection, p. 100.

It is evident that we are dealing with a highly complex history of traditions. There are some points in which all the stories agree. In addition, two sets of parallels stand out.
1) Parallels between the story of Mattathias and that of the mother and her sons.
2) Parallels between the Taxo story and that of Mattathias. In fact the only element in the Taxo story which has its counterpart in 2 Macc 7 rather than in 1 Macc 2 is the number seven, which, as Collins has indicated, could be construed as typological.

A third set of parallels do not occur in the chart, viz., the manner in which both 2 Macc 7 and the Taxo story relate to the last chapters of Deuteronomy. TM is explicitly a rewriting of these chapters. 2 Macc 3-8 utilizes the same historical scheme to describe the same historical events, and the protagonists explicitly cite and quote the Song of Moses as evidence that God is about to have compassion once more on his people (2 Macc 7:6). Moreover, in each document, the story in question forms the turning point from the sin stage to the salvation stage of the historical drama. The Deuteronomic historical scheme does not occur in 1 Maccabees, although the Mattathias story occupies a place analogous to that of the mother and her sons, viz., after the beginning of the persecution and before the victories of Judas. Similarly, the Mattathias story makes no explicit reference to Deuteronomy; however, Mattathias' call for vengeance uses the language of Deut 32:41,43 (1 Macc 2:67f.).

There are two evident explanations of the interdependence of the three stories in question. 1) The Taxo story has developed from the Mattathias story, conflating it with the cave stories in the same chapter; and TM has drawn on the Deuteronomic scheme in 2 Maccabees. 2) The stories in 1 Macc 2 and 2 Macc 7 are in some sense dependent on the Taxo story and its context.

I opt for the latter. The author has produced a rewritten version of the last chapters of Deuteronomy, fleshing out its historical scheme with the events of his own time, using the Taxo story as the trigger that will bring on an imminent theophany, a repetition of Sinai (àla Deut 33), which will constitute the final act of the Deuteronomic scheme. In 1 Macc 2, the action of Mattathias and his injunction to his sons constitutes the turning point that leads to the salvation of Israel. In keeping with his purpose of proclaiming the gospel of the Hasmonaeans, the author recasts the story of the father and his sons, applying it to that father and his sons who did, in point of historical fact, bring deliverance from Antiochus' persecution. Because the author's interest is elsewhere, there remains only a vague verbal allusion to the words of Deuteronomy. In 2 Maccabees, the author makes the most of the Deuteronomic scheme, explaining how it was that persecution befell God's people. He utilizes the story of the mother and her sons as the turning point that leads to Israel's salvation and explicitly cites the Song of Moses to make his point. While he must admit that the victories of Judas did, in in point of historical fact, bring salvation to Israel, he prefaces those victories with the story of the hasidic martyrs, which is the presupposition for those stories and the <u>effective</u> turning point in the historical drama. In short, apocalyptic expectation (as witnessed in the Taxo story) is transformed by the facts of history. God's vindication of his people, originally described in the mythical terms of an expected theophany, is now seen to have happened in the historical facts of Judas' victories over the Seleucid armies.[8]

If we accept the priority of the Mattathias story, we must suppose that allusion to Deuteronomy has become increasingly explicit in 2 Maccabees and TM. In fact, unique similarities between 1 Macc 2 and 2 Macc 7 force us to posit some sort of common source, which I take to be closely related to TM.[9]

d) The affinities of TM with other documents of the 2nd century

In themselves, these affinities are inconclusive for the dating of TM. What I have noted as primitive (pre-Danielic) features in the judgment scene in TM 10 could have been introduced into a late document from an earlier source.[10] By the same token, the parallels to later documents cited by Collins need not indicate a late date for TM.

The Purpose of the Testament of Moses

Collins suggests that TM was composed as a kind of pacifist tract intended to counter "the popular ideology of violent revolution which had been pioneered by Mattathias and which was to bring disaster on Judaism in the first century A.D. Now this anti-militant purpose is not explicit in the text itself. It is a deduction based on the supposition of a late date.

If we accept an early date, we may suggest another purpose, equally in keeping with the text. In her paper on the testament form in TM, Anitra Kolenkow has called attention to our author's repeated concern with the gentiles and their relation to God's plan. As instruments of God's judgment, they will attack Israel, and ignorant of his purpose, they will suppose that they can destroy her. But total annihilation is not permitted, for God will "go forth" to punish the gentiles (12:12f.).[11] This assertion appears to reflect a concern over the survival of Israel. Such a concern is amply attested at the time of Antiochus' persecution (cf. 1 Macc 2:40). In the face of such a concern, TM is encouraging a disheartened people with the promise of divine vindication, viz., that the Lord will yet act to avenge the death of his martyrs and to usher in the end-time and exalt Israel to the heavens.

That a revised version of TM could have been intended to serve the purpose suggested by Collins, I find quite plausible.

---

[8]On the historical tendencies in 1 and 2 Maccabees, see my article, "1 and 2 Maccabees--Same Story, Different Meaning," CTM 42 (1971), 515-26.

[9]That is, 1 Macc 2 and 2 Macc 7 reflect a common source which has certain items peculiar to these two stories. It also knows the Deuteronomic scheme, I suggest, and it has many points in common with TM. The question is whether TM has derived from that source (or 1 Macc 2) or whether that source is derivative from TM. In view of the apocalyptic tenor of TM, which I consider primitive, I suggest the latter alternative.

[10]For these primitive features, see Nickelsburg, Resurrection, pp. 29ff.

[11]Unfortunately, the text in 12:13 breaks off in the middle of the sentence; however, the verb is the same as in 10:3, and we may presume in 12:13 a reference to the act of vengeance described in 10:3.

SOME REMAINING TRADITIO-HISTORICAL PROBLEMS

IN THE TESTAMENT OF MOSES

John J. Collins

In my paper I have proceeded on the principle that we assume the unity of the book unless the contrary is proven. Accordingly I have undertaken to argue the coherence and purposefulness of the book in its present form. My description of its purpose is no less tenable for a redactor in 4 B.C. than it is for an original author. Redactors, too, write with a purpose, and whether we have here a redactor or not, we must explain the book in its present form.

The document as promulgated after the death of Herod obviously had in mind the events of the time of Antiochus. If we accept that the document in its present form dates from about 4 B.C., reference to Maccabean times was almost inevitable. Not only was Judaea in tumult and threatened by a gentile army which destroyed part of the temple, but there was a series of popular insurrections led by first Judas and Mathias, who attempted to pull down the golden eagle,[1] then Judas in Galilee,[2] and Simon in Peraea.[3] Even if we grant that those were common Jewish names, in no way confined to Zealots, the emergence of militant leaders with those names at a time when the law, temple and people were threatened by a gentile army must have brought the Maccabees vividly to mind. The logic of resistance at this period, as expressed by the doctors of the law who tried to pull down the golden eagle, is reminiscent of 2 Macc 7.[4] The ideology of TM may have coincided fairly well with that of the two doctors of the law, who do not appear to have resisted the soldiers, but it must have clashed with the ideology of Judas, Simon and Athronges. Even if an original form of the book in Antiochan times was not specifically anti-militant, it must have taken on such a character at a time when Maccabean traditions were being used in the cause of militancy.

---

[1] Ant. 17.6,2-3 (149-63); JW 1.33,2-4 (651-54). The reference to exaltation over the eagle in TM 10:8 could have acquired special significance in the light of this incident.

[2] Ant. 17.10,5 (271-72); JW 2.4,1 (56).

[3] Ant. 17.10,6 (273-77); JW 2.4,2 (57-59). Another movement at this time was led by Athronges, Ant. 17.10,7 (278-84); JW 2.4,3 (60-65). While any identification of this "mere shepherd" who "had the temerity to aspire to the throne" must be completely hypothetical, Farmer has raised the interesting possibility that he had or claimed some legitimacy as king by Hasmonean descent (see my paper, above, n. 69).

[4] JW 1.33,2 (650): "it was a noble deed to die for the law of one's country; for the souls of those who came to such an end attained immortality and an eternally abiding sense of felicity " (Cf. 2 Macc 7:9).
More especially note how in the following section, 1.33,3 (651-53), the youths are brought before the king: "Who ordered you to do so?" he continued. "The law of our fathers." "And why so exultant, when you will shortly be put to death?" "Because, after our death, we shall enjoy greater felicity."

The present form of TM fits, then, as a coherent and purposeful work in the context of 4 B.C. It was a pacifistic statement, but its pacifism was based on a real expectation of divine vengeance. Irrespective of whether or not the present form is a redaction, the concern for the survival of the nation,[5] the attitude toward the nations, and the desire and expectation of vengeance for the deaths of the martyrs[6] are all entirely appropriate in the context of 4 B.C.

The problem is then: if a redactor could promulgate a work in which at least some specific details of the Antiochan persecution appear not as a punishment for the Hellenizers, but as part of an eschatological punishment, could this apparent distortion of history also have been the work of an original author?[7] Or, rather, is the distortion more easily explained if we posit an earlier stage? Perhaps it is. The specificity of the parallels to the Antiochan persecution is most easily understood if the account is historical. The degree of specificity found here is highly unusual, on any interpretation, and is not really paralleled in the passages cited by Nickelsburg, but is also, as he points out, significantly different from other lists of eschatological woes.[8] The elision of chs 6 and 7 would give a very neat and historical sequence of sin and punishment. I have some reservations on the neatness with which the apocalyptist used the pattern,[9] but I find Nickelsburg's argument at this point persuasive.

I concede, then, that the use of Antiochan material as an eschatological tableau in the present form of TM is more easily explained if it figured in its proper historical sequence in an earlier form of the book. The possibility that the present form is original cannot be completely excluded, but Nickelsburg's

---

[5]It is curious that in TM 12:12 the people who will be punished but will not be utterly destroyed by the nations are "those who sin and set at nought the commandments." In the context of 4 B.C., I would argue, this refers to the militant Jews.

[6]This point is particularly well illustrated by the clamor for vengeance at the funeral of the two doctors of the law, JW 2.1,2 (6-7). Notice, too, how the corruption of the priesthood and cult is raised as an issue.

[7]The possibility can hardly be disputed, but is not of itself of great significance.

[8]The apocalyptic passage which most closely parallels the degree of specificity here is probably Mark 13:9-13: "for they will deliver you up to councils, and you will be beaten in synagogues" etc. This probably reflects conditions already in existence when the evangelist wrote, and which he expected to continue. By analogy we would expect the specific details in TM 8 to refer to conditions in the author's own time. The analogy is not necessarily decisive but there is little other apt comparative material.

[9]In TM 5:1 we read of kings "who share in their guilt and punish them," and since this evidently refers to more than Antiochus Epiphanes, it implies that there was punishment even before the Hellenizers. Sin and punishment may alternate several times, and even to some extent overlap. The second visitation in 8:1 and 9:2 means a visitation comparable to the Babylonian exile, while the other punishments were of lesser significance.

argument from the specificity of the material carries the balance of probability. However, there are a number of points which require further clarification if we accept the Antiochan stage.

Some of the problems concern Nickelsburg's reconstruction of the tradition of the Taxo story. He claims that "unique similarities between 1 Macc 2 and 2 Macc 7" force us to posit a common source which he takes "to be closely related to TM." But most of the similarities which he lists are not paralleled in TM, and so he is forced to posit another, otherwise unknown, source which combines the Taxo story with the common elements of 1 and 2 Macc.[10] The development postulated between TM and 2 Macc is considerable. The only common elements are the number 7 and the fact of martyrdom. The omission of the cave in 2 Maccabees is surprising, especially since the martyrdom in the caves is noted but passed over in virtual silence in 2 Macc 6:11. The substitution of the mother for the father is also difficult. Nickelsburg has given a good explanation of the relevance of the mother, but posits the combination of the motif of Mother Sion with another story of the martyrdom of mothers during the Antiochan persecution before the mother was introduced into the Taxo story, which by then had become the story of seven brothers. If the number seven is, then, the only distinctive feature of the Taxo story which survives in 2 Macc 7, I wonder whether we are justified in positing such a complicated history of the tradition, and whether it would not be simpler to suppose that, at most, only the stereotyped number seven was transferred from the one story to the other.[11] I have seen no convincing argument for deriving Eleazar of 2 Macc 6 from the Taxo story.

The main connection between 2 Macc 7 and TM is their common use of a Deuteronomic schema. The pattern: sin - punishment- turning point - salvation is probably basic to all primitive religion in some form. Sin is punished by plague. Sacrifice is offered. Plague is lifted. The significance which we can attach to the use of this pattern depends largely on the presence or absence of particular motifs, or the dependence on a particular formulation. Now it is virtually certain that Deut 32 underlies both 2 Macc 7 and TM.

The pattern in Deut 32 may be described as follows:

---

[10] The common source can hardly have been Jason of Cyrene, as 2 Maccabees is probably faithful to him, and in 2 Maccabees such motifs of the Taxo story as appear are transferred to the seven brothers. If we accept Tcherikover's opinion that Jason was a contemporary of Judas Maccabaeus (which may, of course, be disputed), we must suppose that the tradition went through three quite distinct phases within ten years. Even this is not impossible, but it further complicates an already complex theory.

[11] The story in *Ant*. 14.15,5 (429-30) may provide a link in the transmission. Like TM 9, it is set in a cave and tells of a father and seven sons. Like 2 Macc 7, there is a confrontation with the king who makes an offer of immunity. However the function and purpose of the story is very different from the other two. The cave setting, at least, is required by the context. In its present truncated form the story can bear no real weight, but if we accept Nickelsburg's reconstruction of the tradition, this story may have a place in it between TM 9 and 2 Macc 7.

1. Israel sins (32:15-18)
2. Punishment (implicitly by the nations) (23-26)
3. This causes hybris among the nations (27-33)
4. So the Lord punishes the nations and takes vengeance for his people (34-43)

There is a somewhat paradoxical shift between points (2) and (4). Israel was being punished by the nations. Yet God takes vengeance for the blood of his servants. Presumably the nations went too far (cf. Isa 10) or Israel was punished too much (cf. Isa 40).

In 2 Macc 7 we find:

1. Israel sins (18, 32)
2. Punishment by Antiochus (18, 32)
3. The king becomes arrogant and tries to fight against God (19, 34, 36)
3a. A prayer in 2 Macc 8:2-3 marks the turning point.
4. The Lord will punish Antiochus (14, 17, 35-37) and take vengeance for the blood of his servants (8:2)

It is debatable here whether the martyrs are the agents who reverse the process of history. 7:38 could be read in the sense that God brings wrath to an end *through* the martyrs (the preposition is *en*), but I think it is more probable that they pray that the wrath will end *with* them. In either case, the prayer in 8:2-3 places the martyrs definitely in the context of the entire persecution. The pollution of the temple, threat to the city and blood of the martyrs mount a cumulative witness against Antiochus. The idea is that the sin of Antiochus and the suffering of the people must reach a certain point and then God acts. When he does, his agent is Judas Maccabaeus.

In TM 2-4 we can also find the pattern of Deut 32:

1. Israel sins (2)
2. Punishment by the nations (3)
3. Prayer, cf. 2 Macc 8:3 (4:1-4)
4. God has compassion on Israel's distress (4:5)

This pattern may also depend on Deut 32, but it is abbreviated. The punishment of the nations and vengeance for the blood are missing, and, as in 2 Macc, a prayer is added.

In TM 5-9 we find:

1. Israel sins (5,7)
2. Punishment by nations (6,8)
3. Deliberate martyrdom by people who are ritually pure (9)
4. The Lord avenges the blood of his servants (9:7)

Two things are striking about the use of the pattern in TM. One is the disparity between the first and second halves. The other is that, unlike either Deuteronomy or 2 Maccabees, a particular act turns the wheel of vengeance. In 2 Maccabees the blood of the martyrs accumulates, with the other elements of the persecution. In TM the rest of the persecution has no effect. The vengeance is brought about solely by the martyrdom of the ritually pure Taxo and his sons.[12]

---

[12] Deut 30:2, to which Nickelsburg points as the model for TM 9 provides an analogy for the idea that there is a positive human role. However, in Deut 30 this role is filled by the repentance of the sinners. In TM 9 there is no mention of repentance, and Taxo and his ancestors are explicitly exempted from the sinfulness of the nation.

Despite the differences, 2 Maccabees and TM both follow the same pattern. However, on my reading, TM has made an innovation in the schema. The human role is no longer merely to draw the Lord's attention to the fact that things have gone far enough. It can actually do something which will get an automatic response from God. This means that Taxo and his sons emerge as the cause of salvation in a more direct way than the seven brothers in 2 Macc 7 and in a way that is not provided for in Deut 32. (This difference must weaken to some extent the link between TM and 2 Maccabees.)

There was another paradigm which could be used in time of persecution which was rather different from Deut 32. In Num 25: 6-13 we find the story of Phineas. It may be set out as follows:

1. Israel sinned
2. Punishment by a plague
3. Phineas acted with zeal
4. The plague was turned away

As Nickelsburg and others have noted, this paradigm is used in 1 Maccabees. It suited the purpose of that author better than Deut 32, because it provided a role for a human hero who directly changed the course of events. Despite the occurrence of the terms *avenge* and *pay back* in 1 Macc 2:67f. (cf. Deut 32:41,43), I do not think that this pattern owes anything to Deut 32.

The significant point which emerges from the comparisons we have made is that TM introduces the element of a human hero into the Deuteronomic pattern. The role of this hero is analogous to that of the hero in the Phineas story and 1 Maccabees, but he uses different methods--suggested by Deut 32. Was this innovation in the form of the story more likely to have been made independently by TM or in deliberate opposition to the Mattathias story? If it was made independently, we can perhaps understand why Mattathias embodies some characteristics of Taxo. However, the absence of Taxo from 2 Maccabees makes it unlikely that the figure in TM 9 was a widely popular hero.

The difference between the application of the Deuteronomic pattern in 2 Maccabees and TM may have some significance in nuancing the theological position of those books. Nickelsburg has tended to group these and some other books together as "Hasidic." If we can validly speak of Hasidic theology, then we will have isolated a rather important strand in Judaism. Accordingly, the notion deserves to be examined with caution. I am not sure that the ideology of TM corresponds so obviously with what we know of the Hasidim. I understand TM as a definitely pacifist document. Taxo and his sons deliberately seek martyrdom. There is no question of resistance, and the resolve to die is made at a point when Taxo and his sons are not yet prisoners as is the case in 2 Macc 7. I am not sure that this was the stance of the "mighty warriors of Israel" described in 1 Macc 2:42. The issue in the time of the Hasidim was war on the sabbath--an issue that troubled Jewish militants on several occasions. On Tcherikover's reconstruction, the Hasidim were the original leaders of armed resistance. The discrepancy is not insuperable, but it suggests that some caution is necessary in the present state of our knowledge of the Hasidim.[13]

---

[13] Perhaps we could suppose the document was written by a Hasid whose teacher/ leader had been killed in the cave massacre. Then the expectation of vengeance to follow the leader's death might make the armed revolt appear insignificant.

Finally, I would like to raise again the problem of TM 4:8, which apparently denies the cultic validity of the second temple. This rejection of the temple is not alleviated by the author's attacks on those who polluted it. The rejection was probably based on the fact that it was polluted. The problematic point is that the rejection is not limited to the time of the Hellenizers or to any such period but covers the whole time from the Return from the exile. This could hardly have been written by one who up to recently had been attached to the official (Zadokite) clergy, as is so often assumed for the Hasidim.[14]

Conclusion

I agree that the unusual specificity of TM 8 makes it probable that this work had an earlier, Antiochan stage. However, this history of the traditions involved, and the interrelation between TM and the books of Maccabees require considerable further clarification. In its present form, from the turn of the era, TM is a coherent and purposeful work. In view of the circumstances of 4 B.C., TM probably took on an anti-militant character which need not be assumed in an earlier stage, written before the rise of the Maccabees.

---

[14] 1 Enoch 89:73 provides an early second century parallel for the rejection of the temple cult. If this passage is considered Hasidic, serious doubts must be raised about the priestly origins of the Hasidim.

THE TESTAMENT OF MOSES: ITS CONTENT, ITS ORIGIN,

AND ITS ATTESTATION IN JOSEPHUS

Jonathan A. Goldstein

1. The Original Content

In periods when God seems to hide himself precious indeed is the word of God to the pious. They are then apt to take their own wishful thinking for divine revelation. False prophesies have often had profound influence in history, and texts of them have much to teach the historian. Disappointed believers, however, tend to suppress the memory of prophesies which prove too obviously to be false. The Testament of Moses, a false prophesy, survives miraculously only in Latin on a corrupt nearly-illegible palimpsest. By suggesting that chs. 6 and 7 are probably an interpolation dating from post-Herodian times, Jacob Licht has provided the key to seeing this text as originally an apocalypse of the time of the persecution of the Jews by Antiochus IV.[1] Licht made his suggestion with the diffidence which is appropriate when one deals with a text so illegible and so obscure. Nevertheless, he is probably right.

The seer of the Testament of Moses proceeded as did the authors of the apocalypses at Enoch 85-90 and Dan 7, 8, and 11, which also come from the time of Antiochus IV:[2] he gave a synoptic view of history down to the time of the persecution. The events immediately preceding and during the persecution are described with such detail as to suggest strongly that these are the events of the situation confronting the author and his intended audience. The authors of the apocalypses in Enoch and Daniel did not invent their predictions. They derived them from "scientific" study of the words of earlier "true prophets," especially Isaiah.[3] Similarly, the author of the Testament of Moses did not invent but derived his predictions especially from Deut 32, Joel, and Isaiah.

All three apocalypses failed to be fulfilled. The apocalypses in Daniel and Enoch were being supplemented, to keep them up-to-date with unexpected events, already during the

---

[1] J. Licht, "Taxo, or the Apocalyptic Doctrine of Vengeance," JJS 12 (1961) 95-103. See also George W. E. Nickelsburg, Jr., Resurrection, Immortality, and Eternal Life in Intertestamental Judaism (HST 26; Cambridge: Harvard University Press, 1972) 43-45.

[2] I shall deal with the Testament of Moses and the apocalypses of Enoch and Daniel in future studies, including Chapter 2 of the introduction to my forthcoming commentary to First and Second Maccabees, to be published in the Anchor Apocrypha.

[3] See Nickelsburg, Resurrection, pp. 17-26; on Enoch 90:20-42, for the present see R. H. Charles, The Book of Enoch (Oxford, 1893), ad loc., and The Apocrypha and Pseudepigrapha of the Old Testament (Oxford, 1913), II, 259-60.

persecutions and during the career of Judas Maccabeaus.[4] Nevertheless those apocalypses proved to be obscure enough so that some of the faithful could preserve them as they were in the lifetime of Judas Maccabeaus, and later believers could interpret the wicked empire as Rome, without changing the text.[5] On the other hand, the Testament of Moses probably was too specific. Taxo the martyr and his seven sons may well have been real persons who were remembered. Their deaths obviously did not bring the predicted miraculous consummation of history. Believers might hold that the victories of the Hasmonaeans were a prelude to the predicted consummation; but when a century elapsed and the Jews were "enslaved" to Rome and the Herodian dynasty, believers could preserve the Testament of Moses as a true prophesy only by altering its text to take account of the unexpected events. A pious reviser could believe that his alterations of the text represented the intent of the original author, but he would have known that not everyone had to agree with him. Suspicious skeptics can exist in any period. To minimize the challenges of skeptics, a pious reviser must make his additions and alterations as slight as possible. He will prefer to place them at positions where it is conceivable that material could have been misread or lost from an original manuscript, such as at the beginning or the end of a scroll or at the foot or the head of a column of writing.[6] Licht suggests that all of the material in chs. 6 and 7 is interpolated. Always bearing in mind the tenuous preservation of the text, we are entitled to ask whether the reviser would have dared to add so much.

Indeed, if all of chs. 6 and 7 represents a later interpolation, a difficulty arises: the seer jumps from describing the impious regime (ca. 175-169) of the corrupt and unjust high priests Jason and Menelaus (ch. 5)[7] to tell of the persecution (ch. 8), without mentioning either Antiochus IV's rapid march in 169 from Egypt to capture Jerusalem and sack the temple or the murderous expedition of Apollonius the Mysarch in 167.[8]

---

[4] Licht's theory of interpolation becomes all the more certain when the development of the Testament of Moses is compared with that of the apocalypses in Enoch and Daniel. I shall analyze the development and carry out the comparisons in the studies mentioned above in n.2.

[5] E.g., Jerome to Dan 7:7; Babylonian Talmud, ʿAbodah zarah 2b. The new temple brought by God (Enoch 90:28-29) is the probable source of a long chain of texts; see those collected by V. Aptowitzer, "The Heavenly Temple in the Agada," Tarbiz 2 (1930-31) 270-72 (Hebrew). Perhaps the falsity of the bulk of Enoch eventually proved to be so blatant that Jews and most Christians abandoned the book and did not attempt to preserve it by interpolation.

[6] Thus, the author of Dan 12:4-end appended the passage to Daniel 11:1-12:3 when it became clear that the death of Antiochus IV did not conform to 11:40-45 and was not followed by the resurrection.

[7] 2 Macc 4:1-10:10.

[8] Charles noticed the omission (AP, II, 420).

The seer's interest in Jerusalem and the temple is such[9] that it is inconceivable that he could have omitted these events. It is likely that the seer alluded to them in his own original version of ch. 6. If our dating of the Testament of Moses is correct, 6:1 is certainly a post-Hasmonaean interpolation. The rest of the chapter, however, may contain the original words of the seer amid post-Herodian alterations. After speaking of the sinful leadership of the high priests in ch. 5, the seer may have gone on in ch. 6 to write,[10]

> There shall come upon them an insolent king, a man rash and wicked,[11] and he shall cut off their chief men with the sword. He shall slay old and young, sparing none.[12] He shall inflict punishment upon them as he did upon the Egyptians.[13] He shall burn a part of their temple with fire.[14]

Thus, the seer, like the authors of 1 and 2 Maccabees, would have viewed Antiochus' sack of Jerusalem as punishment for the sins of

---

[9] See 2:4,6; 3:2; 4:7-8; 5:3-4,6,9; 8:5. Dan 7 probably does not mention the events before the persecution, but that apocalypse is a reworking of an earlier prophesy which mentioned neither Jerusalem nor the temple, as I shall show. The author of the apocalypse in Enoch had a negative attitude toward the second temple. See below.

[10] The Latin text would be as follows, with brackets around the probable interpolations: *Et succedit illis rex petulans [qui non erit de genere sacerdotum], homo temerarius et improbus, qui elidit principales eorum gladio [et locis ignotis singuli et corpora illorum, ut nemo sciat, ubi sint corpora illorum]. Occidit maiores natu et iuuenes non parcet. [Tunc timor erit illius aceruus in eis in terram eorum] et faciet in eis iudicia, quomodo fecit in Aegyptiis.* For the last three words, the palimpsest has *fecerunt in illis Aegypti*, which I take to be the reviser's effort to make my hypothetical original text fit Herod.

The Latin continues: *[per xxx et iiii annos et puniunt eos et producit natos . . . ecedentes sibi breuiora tempora dominarent* (palimpsest: *donarent)].* I omit here the next words, which may refer to the expedition of the Mysarch (see below, n. 16) and pass to words which may have been transposed from their original position by the reviser: *et partem aedis ipsorum igni incendit.*

[11] Cf. 1 Macc 1:10; 2 Macc 5:15,17,21; 9:4,7-8; Dan 8:23.

[12] Cf. 1 Macc 1:20; 2 Macc 5:11-14; Dan 11:28. 1 Macc 1:20 is defective and can be restored from Josephus Ant. 12.5,3-4 (246b-247a, 249). The meaning of Dan 11:28 is not obvious but can be shown to be relevant. I prove these assertions in my forthcoming commentary, to 1 Macc 1:20.

[13] See 1 Macc 1:17, to be compared with 1:20 as restored from Josephus (see above, n.12); and Dan 11:25-26, to be compared with 11:28 as interpreted above in n.12.

[14] See 2 Macc 1:8 and 8:33. Though the pious authors in 2 Maccabees blamed Jason and his men for the fire, clearly it was set in the course of Antiochus IV's attack, so he, too, could be blamed for it.

Jason and Menelaus and the members of their factions.[15] In 6:8 the seer may have gone on to speak of the expedition of the Mysarch,

> Into their country the murdering troops of a powerful king shall come, who shall conquer them and carry off captives.[16]

Even if all of 6:1-7 might belong to the interpolator, v.8 might still be read as referring to Antiochus IV's capture and sack of Jerusalem:

> Into their country murdering troops shall come and a powerful king, who shall conquer them and carry off captives and burn part of their temple.[17]

The intelligible part of ch. 7 deals with impious gluttonous men of power of a sort not mentioned in the historical sources reflecting the time between the expedition of the Mysarch and the publication of Antiochus IV's decrees against Jewish religious observance. Hence, all of ch. 7 may be post-Herodian interpolation.

If our reconstruction is correct, the words of the seer contain the reactions of a contemporary to the wickedness of the high priests who defiled the temple, to Antiochus IV's capture and sack of Jerusalem and the burning of part of the temple (presumably, a gate),[18] to the expedition of the Mysarch (probably), and to the persecution including the imposition of the idolatrous cult. These are the last important historical events known to the original author, who says nothing of pious armed resistance to Antiochus IV. Hence, our seer wrote early in the persecution, in winter or spring of 167/6 B.C.[19]

2. Attestation of the Text in Josephus

Our seer's prophesy, even when brought up to date in post-Herodian times, proved to be false. Yet his words survived long. Since they were placed in the mouth of Moses, they were probably written in Hebrew. They survived to be translated into Greek and

---

[15] 1 Macc 1:11-15,28; 2 Macc 1:7; 4:10-17; 5:17-20.

[16] *In partes* (palimpsest: *pares*) *eorum cohortes* (palimpsest: *mortis*) *uenient occidentes* (palimpsest: *et occidentes*) *regis potentis* (palimpsest: *rex potens*) *qui* (palimpsest: *quia*) *expugnabunt* (palimpsest: *expugnabit*) *eos et ducent captiuos*. By changing *rex potens* of the palimpsest to the genitive or by regarding it as a mistranslated Hebrew *nomen rectum* in a construct-phrase, we make sense of the interpolator's version: the Roman soldiers who hit Jerusalem hard in quelling a rebellion in 4 B.C. (Josephus Ant. 17.10,1-11,1 (250-299) served the "king" Augustus, but Augustus was not present.

[17] Latin as in n.16, except for reading *occidentes et rex potens* here. The last words of the chapter, *aliquos crucifigit circa coloniam eorum*, probably belong to the interpolator (see Josephus Ant. 17.10,10 (295). No crucifixions are reported in connection with Antiochus' expedition in 169 or with that of the Mysarch.

[18] See above, n. 14.

[19] See 1 Macc 1:54.

the Greek to be translated into our extant Latin text. Can it be that no other surviving Jewish work took note of the Testament of Moses? The influence of our seer's words may be reflected in 1 Macc 2:29-38 and in 2 Macc 6:11, but there is no way of showing that the author of either book read our seer's work.

Josephus, however, was a proud believer in the veracity of Jewish prophesy, especially that of Daniel.[20] If the Testament of Moses could have been translated into Latin, it also could have reached the eyes of Josephus. There is more than one indication that Josephus knew the Testament of Moses.

Writing of the Zealots at JW 2.8,3 (388), Josephus says,

> There was an ancient saying of inspired men that the city would fall and the sanctuary would be burnt according to the laws of war when civil strife shall befall the city and native hands shall be the first to defile God's sacred precinct. This saying the Zealots did not disbelieve, yet they voluntarily fulfilled it.

Our seer predicts that high priests will defile the temple (5:3-4) and that dissension and injustice will prevail in Jerusalem (5:2-6), surely to the point of constituting the civil strife described in detail in 2 Macc 4:1-5:10. The "chief men" of Test Mos 6:3 could well include chief men of the feuding factions. At Test Mos 6:9 there is a prediction that part of the temple will be burnt. No other text is known from which Josephus could have derived his "saying of inspired men." Hence, there is a good chance that he derived it from the Testament of Moses. If so, we learn also that Josephus and the Zealots accepted our seer's work as inspired. Indeed, in its present version, Test Mos 6:8-9 lends itself to being read as a description of the conquest of Jerusalem by Vespasian and Titus.

Another possible allusion to our seer's work stands at Josephus Ant. 12.5,4 (256). There, Josephus appears to be drawing on both 1 and 2 Maccabees, but neither source says, as does Josephus, that crucifixion was the punishment for violation of the ban on circumcision. That fact appears only at Test Mos 8:1.

3. The Sect to which the Author Belonged.

To what group of Jews did our seer belong? Josephus and the Zealots could be eclectic in dealing with earlier sectarian literature, so that we cannot identify the author's position with that of Josephus; the seer's ideology of martyrdom certainly does not qualify him to be a proto-Zealot. Taxo, however, resembles the pietist martyrs of 1 Macc 2:29-38 and 2 Macc 6:11, who probably called themselves H^asidim.[21]

One passage in our seer's work is very strange and may be important for identifying his sect. At 4:6 the seer alludes to Cyrus' decree allowing the return to the exiles. At 4:7 he goes on to say,

---

[20] See Josephus Ant. 10,11,7 (267-81); 12.7,6 (322).

[21] See 1 Macc 2:42.

Then some parts of the tribes will go up and return to their appointed place, and they shall build it anew and surround it with walls.[22]

Our author may be drawing on Isa 61:4 (especially in his expression "build anew"), as if he saw the prophesy there partly fulfilled in the events. If so, he saw only partial fulfillment, for he goes on to say in v.8,

Only two tribes will remain steadfast in their established (?) faith, grieved and groaning because they will not be able to offer up sacrifices to the Lord of their fathers.[23]

The seer probably took "grieved and groaning" from Ezek 9:4, where the words refer to the scrupulous minority, scandalized over the abominations of the majority. However, at this point the seer mentions no abominations. Yet, as we have his words, he says that even after the building of the second temple and after Nehemiah's walling of Jerusalem, scrupulous Jews of the two tribes who returned from exile will still be unable to offer up sacrifices to their God! Unlike the seer of Enoch 89:73, our author says nothing of violations of the laws of purity which might have made the sacrifices invalid. If we take him literally, he here denies the cultic validity of the second temple!

We may be sure that there were Jews who so rejected the second temple and did so on the basis of Deut 12:8-14, Isa 66:1-3, Jer 7:3-15, Ezek 24:21, and Lam 2:7. Though a miracle had attested God's election of Solomon's temple (2 Chr 7:1-3), no miracle had yet attested His election of the second temple.[24] But our author accepted the book of Ezra-Nehemiah and bitterly complained when wicked priests and gentiles violated the second temple. In contrast, the author of Enoch 90:6-18 says nothing about desecrations of the temple, complaining only of the slaughter of Israelites. The absence of the temple from our seer's description of the glorious End is not significant. If he believed that Israel was to be raised to heaven, he must also have believed that the temple would be, too, in accordance with Isa 2:2 and Mic 4:1. Our seer and his audience took Isa 2 and Mic 4 for granted. Therefore he had no need to mention the future of the temple. It was the sectarian author of Enoch 90:28-29 who had to mention it, for he was teaching the relatively new doctrine, that the second temple would be replaced by a new structure brought by God himself. Hence, we may be sure that for our seer the second temple is not to be replaced; it is good enough.

What, then, should we make of our seer's statement which seems to deny the cultic validity of the second temple? Either a word has fallen out, presumably a translation of Hebrew l^{e}rason, "acceptably," or else, for our seer "to offer up sacrifices" by itself meant "to offer up sacrifices acceptably" in the sense

---

[22]*Tunc ascendent aliquae partes tribuum et uenient in locum constitutum suum et circumuallabunt locum renouantes.*

[23]*Duae autem tribus permanebunt in praeposita fide sua, tristes et gementes, quia non poterint referre immolationes domino patruum suorum.*

[24]See Ezra 3, 6. The purpose of the legends at 2 Macc 1:19-2:8 is to deny or explain away charges that the second temple was not fully God's chosen place. See my forthcoming commentary.

that God would respond to them with miracles.[25] The rabbis, heirs of the Pharisees, were well aware of how the second temple lacked important sacred attributes even while they revered it.[26] Thus, our seer could well have been a proto-Pharisee.

We can be quite certain that our author does not stand in the tradition of the Essenes of Qumran with their sectarian solar calendar and its 364-day year and its 49-year Jubilee.[27] At Jub 50:4 the time of Israel's entry into Canaan and Moses' death is placed in the fiftieth 49-year Jubilee, in the year of creation 2450. Our seer places the death of Moses in the year of creation 2500, in the fiftieth 50-year Jubilee (1:2). On the other hand, the apocalypse of Enoch 85-90 is intimately connected with the tradition of the Essenes of Qumran and their calendar. It stands with the study of that calendar at Enoch 72-82, and the sectarian author of Jub 4:18-20 alludes to the apocalypse. The Enoch apocalypse thus may well represent proto-Essenes who admired Judas Maccabaeus.[28]

4. The Kings at 2:7 and the Speaker of the Prayer at 4:1-4

We all owe a debt of gratitude to R. H. Charles, whose commentary first opened up many of the secrets of our text. However, one way of showing gratitude is to improve upon his foundation. At 2:6 Charles perceived that our seer was discussing the twenty rulers of the southern kingdom, including Athaliah. We may improve upon Charles' translation as follows:

Seven shall build walls round about, and I shall beset nine, but ⟨four⟩ shall violate the covenant of God . . . .

Besides mistranslating "beset" as "protect,"[29] Charles divided the rulers of Judah into three groups in arbitrary fashion, of the rise, of the period of power, and of the decline. In fact, the Biblical histories reveal a far more complex pattern of ups and downs. Rather, the seer has accepted the judgments passed on the rulers by the Chronicler. Seven were largely righteous: Abijah, Asa, Jehoshaphat, Uzziah, Jotham, Hezekiah, and Josiah; they built moral and physical walls to strengthen Israel (cf. Ezek 23:30, Ezra 9:9, and Mishnah Abot 1:1). Nine sinned enough to be beset by divine chastisement: Rehoboam, Jehoram, Ahaziah, Joash, Amaziah, Jehoahaz, Jehoiakim, Jehoiachin, and Zedekiah. Four were so wicked as to be outright idolaters: Athaliah, Ahaz, Menasseh, and Amon.

---

[25] See Ezek 20:41-44 and Mal 1:10-13 and 3:4 in the context of its entire chapter; Ps 51:18-21.

[26] See Louis Ginzberg, Legends of the Jews (Philadelphia, 1928) 6, 377-78, n. 118, and my forthcoming commentary to 2 Macc 1:19-2:8.

[27] See Shemaryahu Talmon, "The Calendar Reckoning of the Sect from the Judaean Desert," Scripta Hierosolymitana 4 (1958) 162-99.

[28] See Chapter 2 of the introduction to my forthcoming commentary.

[29] For circumibo here as "beset, cf. Ps 59 (58):15 and Ps 88 (87):18 in the Hebrew, the Greek versions, and the Vulgate.

Charles jumps to the conclusion that the speaker of the
prayer at 4:1-4 is Daniel. I shall show elsewhere that Dan 9
was written after the Testament of Moses. Nothing suggests any
connection between the prayer in Dan 9 and the prayer here in
Test Mos 4:1-4. Rather, if the speaker of the prayer is human,
he would be Isaiah, who did utter prayers for Israel (25-26;
27:4; 63:7-64:12). Our author readily uses the Hebrew expressions
of his own time,[30] but he still draws heavily on Isaiah. The
"King on the lofty throne" comes from Isa 6:1. "That this
people should be your chosen people" probably reflects Isa 43:20;
45:4. "Round about ⟨shall be⟩ the gate of foreigners and the
place where there is vast pride," may well mean that the
Israelites will be enclosed by the gates of Babylon ("Bab-El"
literally means "Gate of God"), the place of pride, as might be
derived from Isa 43:14; 62:10 and 13:19. "Look down and have compassion
upon them, heavenly Lord," reflects Isa 63:15. However,
the seer probably intended that the speaker of the prayer should
be taken as an angel. He calls the speaker "one who is in charge
of (or "concerned with") them," an expression which is never used
of a prophet but appears to be taken from Job 33:23, "If there
be concerned with him an angel, a mediator, one of a thousand . .
. ." ('im yēš 'ālāw mal'āk mēlīṣ 'eḥad minnī 'ālep), where the
request of the angel is said to bring God's salvation upon the
sufferer. The expression "who is in charge of" ('ªšer 'al) is
also regularly used of royal ministers and hence is appropriate
for ministering angels.[31] Angels also defend Israel's cause at
Dan 10:13, 21 and at Enoch 89:77.

5. The Meaning and Original Text of 8:4-5

There can be no doubt that all of ch. 8 deals with the persecution
and the imposed idolatrous cult. One would expect the
climax to come in v. 5 with a reference to the Abomination of
Desolation. However, 8:5 appears to be incoherent and unintelligible.
The Latin text of 8:4-5 has

> Nam illi in eis punientur in tormentis et igne et ferro, et
> cogentur palam baiulare idola eorum, inquinata quomodo sunt
> pariter continentibus ea. Et a torquentibus illos pariter
> cogentur intrare in abditum locum eorum et cogentur stimulis
> blasfemare uerbum contumeliose, nouissime post haec et leges
> quod haberent supra altarium suum.

The words following the last comma are ungrammatical, for a neuter
singular relative pronoun has as its apparent antecedent a feminine
plural noun, and a verb in the imperfect subjunctive follows
a main verb in the future indicative. Perhaps we may ascribe the
irregular sequence of tenses to the inelegant Latin translator.
The long sequence of verbs listing the dreadful acts which Jews
will be compelled to perform suggests that yet another verb
should stand where leges ("laws") does, perhaps locare or ligare
("place," "affix"). If so, we may translate the passage,

---

[30]See Avi Hurwitz, "Adon Hakkol," Tarbiz 34 (1964-65) 224-27
(Hebrew).

[31]1 Kgs 12:18; 2 Kgs 18:18; Isa 22:15, etc. Alternatively,
a royal minister is called śar- ("chief of . . ."), as are the
angels at Dan 10:20-21; see, e.g., Gen 21:22; 37:36. For an
angel making a request similar to Test Mos 4:1-4, cf. Zech 1:12,
G.N.

For therein they shall be punished with tortures and fire
and sword and shall be forced publicly to haul their idols,
polluted as they are like those who hold them. By their
torturers they shall be compelled to enter their secret
place (sc. the Holy of Holies), and by whips they shall
be compelled to blaspheme the Word with abusive language,
and finally, after these atrocities, even to place over
their altar that which they were holding.

Antiochus' act of desecration was all the more heinous because
he made Jews haul the idolatrous objects and fasten them
to the temple altar.[32]

Jonathan A. Goldstein
University of Iowa
Iowa City, Iowa 52242

---

[32] See Babylonian Talmud, Abodah zarah 42a (statement of Raba) and Mishnah, Abodah zarah 3:5, and see also my forthcoming commentary to 1 Macc 1:54-59.

THE ASSUMPTION OF MOSES AND JEWISH HISTORY:
4 B.C. - A.D. 48[1].
David M. Rhoads

Emil Schürer considered that the author of the Assumption of Moses (AM) was to be sought for "among the Zealots."[2] Although his viewpoint has not been generally accepted, it would be helpful to reconsider the evidence for a Zealot authorship, and to ask what our study might contribute to an understanding of the period in which it probably was written (4 B.C. - A.D. 30).[3]

Schürer placed the author within the ranks of the Zealots because he found it impossible to place his party affiliation within the other three main Jewish sects of the first century--the Sadducees, Pharisees, and Essenes. He concluded that since the author could not be identified with these sects, he must have been an adherent of the fourth main sect, the Zealots. However, such an argument was based on an outmoded view of first-century Judaism, which neatly divided Palestinian Jews into four sects.

The discovery of the Dead Sea Scrolls has dramatically brought about a revision of our understanding of first-century Judaism. Along with other previously recognized factors in first-century Palestine, the Hellenistic influences evident there prohibit any attempt to see Palestinian Judaism as isolated from outside influence. And the mere presence of a sect at Qumran emphasizes anew the variety of groups which must have characterized this period. Perhaps Morton Smith's writings, especially his article on "Palestinian Judaism in

---

[1]I would like to acknowledge the helpful suggestions of Dr. James Charlesworth and Dr. W. D. Davies, both of Duke University, in the preparation of this paper.

[2]Emil Schürer, A History of the Jewish People in the Time of Jesus Christ, Division I, Volume 2 (Edinburgh: T. and T. Clark, 1901), pp. 73-83.

[3]R. H. Charles, in his introduction to AM (The Apocrypha and Pseudepigrapha of the Old Testament in English, Volume 2 [Oxford: Clarendon Press, 1913], p. 411), has stated the classic position regarding its date. He argues that AM 1:17 presupposes that the temple is still standing, which implies a time of writing which precedes A.D. 70. AM 6:7 refers to the death of Herod the Great. AM 6:9 mentions the War of Varus. Since both events took place in 4 B.C., the writing must post-date that year. Further, AM 6:7 states that "he [Herod] shall beget children, [who] suceeding him shall rule for shorter periods." This may have been written shortly after 4 B.C. to prophesy a speedy end for the offspring of a wicked king. More likely, it was written after A.D. 6, when one of Herod's sons, Archelaus, was deposed by the Romans after a brief reign of ten years. This assertion about the short reigns of Herod's sons would not have been written after A.D. 30 when two of Herod's sons, Philip and Antipas, would have already enjoyed reigns the length of their father's. Hence, AM may have been written any time between 4 B.C. and A.D. 30, but it was most likely penned in the period shortly after A.D. 6.

Palestine is widely presupposed as the provenance for AM. See, for example, Torrey, The Apocryphal Literature (London: H. Milford, 1945), p. 116; and Eissfeldt, The Old Testament, trans. by Peter Ackroyd (Oxford: B. Blackwell, 1965), p. 624.

the First Century,"[4] best illustrates the new point of view concerning the diversity within Judaism in the years before the Roman-Jewish War of A.D. 66-73. W. D. Davies has long exposed the false dichotomy between Semitic or Palestinian Judaism and Hellenistic or Diaspora Judaism.[5] And Neusner's recent studies of the Pharisees have demonstrated that the Pharisaic sect may have been smaller, less significant and yet more heterogeneous than it has been traditionally pictured.[6] Surely the options open for characterizing the author of AM are not limited to the major sects traditionally known to us. Certainly, Schürer's basis for identifying him as a Zealot are dubious on these grounds alone.

Perhaps more important, however, is the fact that recent studies have also shown that probably there was not a sect called by the name "Zealot" during the early first century.[7] The title has been traditionally associated with the revolutionary sect founded by Judas of Galilee in A.D. 6. However, Josephus' reports of the founding of a sect by Judas give it no name (War 2:118; Antiquities 18:9-10, 23-25). Lake pointed out long ago that Josephus limits the use of "Zealot" as a party name to the extremist faction in Jerusalem from A.D. 68-70, which was formed to overthrow the moderate Jewish government and to guarantee the active prosecution of the war.[8] In the years before the war, there may have been Jewish Zealots such as Simon the zealot (the disciple of Jesus) and Paul (who refers to himself as a zealot with respect to his persecution of the church); but M. Borg has shown that there is no evidence for the use of the term "Zealot" as a party name before the war period (that is, before A.D. 66).[9] Clearly, it would be mistaken to identify the author of AM as a Zealot if there were no such sect in existence at the time of his writing, early in the first century.

Although it did not bear the name "Zealot," there may

---

[4]In Israel: Its Role in Civilization, ed. by Moshe Davis (New York: The Seminary Israel Institute, 1956).

[5]See Especially "Reflexions on Tradition: The Aboth Revisited" in Christian History and Interpretation: Studies Presented to John Knox, ed. by W. R. Farmer et. al. (Cambridge: University Press, 1967), pp. 138-151.

[6]J. Neusner, The Rabbinic Traditions about the Pharisees before 70 (3 vols.; Leiden: Brill, 1971); From Politics to Piety (Englewood Cliffs: Prentice Hall, 1971); and "Josephus' Pharisees," Ex Orbe Religionum, Studia Geo Widengren Oblata, Vol. I (Leiden, 1972).

[7]G. Baumbach, "Zeloten und Sicarier: ihre geschichtliche und religionspolitische Bedeutung," Bibel und Liturgie, 41 (1968), 2-25; Marc Borg, "The Currency of the term 'Zealot,'" Journal of Theological Studies, 22 (1971), 504-512; Morton Smith, "Zealots and Sicarii, Their Origins and Relation," Harvard Theological Review, 64 (1971), 1-19; S. Zeitlin, "Zealots and Sicarii," Journal of Biblical Literature, 81 (1962), 395-398.

[8]In his appendix on the "Zealots" in The Beginnings of Christianity, vol. I (London: Macmillan, 1920).

[9]"The Currency of the Term 'Zealot,'" Journal of Theological Studies, 22 (1971), 504-512.

have been a revolutionary sect at the time of the writing of AM. It may have been Schürer's intention to identify the author with this sect--in spite of a traditional misuse of the title "Zealot." Josephus asserts that Judas the Galilaean founded such a sect in A.D. 6. It is possible to connect Judas' teaching of "No lord but God" and his descendants (Menahem and Eleazar ben Jair) with the later revolutionary sect which Josephus identifies as the "Sicarii." The Sicarii emerged (in Josephus' narrative) at the opening of the war period and,[10] after being expelled from Jerusalem by another revolutionary faction, they spent the remainder of the war years until A.D. 73 on the fortress Masada. Several factors, however, suggest that this revolutionary sect came into existence only around the last two decades before the war. Josephus' accounts of the founding of a sect by Judas in A.D. 6 are fraught with contradictions and problems; and in those accounts, the sect is given no title. Further, Josephus records no conspiratorial revolutionary activity in Palestine between A.D. 6 and A.D. 48. When he gives an account of the revolutionaries who were active in the 50's and 60's before the war period, Josephus gives no evidence of the presence of a sect or unified movement. Rather, the revolutionary activity of these two decades before the war seems to have been the result of a variety of social, political and economic dissatisfactions. Expressions of violence were mainly local and sporadic. In addition, Josephus' attempts to attribute the founding of a sect to Judas of Galilee in A.D. 6 may simply have been a function of his apologetic desire to blame the war upon a small group of innovative Jews--thereby exonerating the Jewish populace as a whole. Thus, although the sect of Sicarii (active in the war years, A.D. 66-73) had definite philosophical and historical roots in Judas the Galilaean, the idea that he founded the sect and that it existed from A.D. 6 is probably an historical retrojection on the part of Josephus.

Hence, it seems unlikely, on the basis of the historical context, that the author of AM might be identified as an adherent of a revolutionary sect.

It is possible, however, to characterize the work as militant, even if it is not to be placed within a revolutionary sect. Torrey argues thus when he identifies the figure of Taxo (Chap. IX) with the person of Mattathias, the father of the Maccabaean movement.[11] As such, the author of AM implies (so Torrey argues) that the ideal action on the part of Jews, which Taxo represents, includes the taking-up of arms on behalf of the Jewish nation. However, this interpretation of Taxo seems unlikely. Taxo exhorts "Let us die rather than transgress the commands of the Lord of Lords, the God of our fathers." It must be conceded that Taxo's outlook is at this point identical with the "original" intention of the followers of Mattathias who went to live in caves where they could pur-

---

[10]Josephus employs the term "Sicarii" as a party title only during the war years (e.g. War 4:400). This is not to be confused with his pre-war references to the sicarii (properly translated with a lower-case "s"; e.g. War 2:254-257). Here the term is applied in its functional meaning to refer to revolutionary brigands who used daggers, or sicae, for political assassinations.

[11]C. C. Torrey, "'Taxo' in the Assumption of Moses," JBL, 62 (1943), 1-7.

sue the law without interference. However, the comparison
stops here. The Maccabeans became disillusioned with the
deaths by persecution which followed their pursuit of the
law, and subsequently they took up arms. The author of the
AM shows nothing of this disillusionment. The figure of Taxo
focuses on the redemptive significance of death by persecution. "If we do this, and die," he says, "our blood will be
avenged before the Lord." (AM 9:7).

The significance which the author attaches to the death
of a figure like Taxo implies a program of non-resistance.
Instead of the active vengeance upon transgressors which is
associated with the zeal of a figure like Phineas, who kills
the offender, a vengeance which results in atonement for the
people of Israel, the author of AM asserts that vengeance is
the work of God alone (10:7). However, God's vengeance against
nations which oppress the Jewish people can be assured if it
is certain that those nations unjustly spilled the blood of
innocent Jews. Licht has shown correctly that the exhortation
by Taxo to retreat to the caves offers the twofold purpose
of assuring absolute obedience (and therefore innocence) by
the followers and of offering an active challenge (passive
resistance) to the authorities to persecute them--an unjust
persecution which God must surely avenge.[12] A parallel alternative in contrast to the atonement wrought by the vengeful
killing by a figure like Phineas is the notion present in the
Dead Sea Scrolls that obedience of the sect to the law will
offer atonement for Israel and result in the punishment of
those nations who are not obedient. Both alternatives (Dead
Sea Scrolls and AM) appear to involve a doctrine of obedient
non-resistance (in the case of AM more appropriately to be
characterized as passive resistance). Vengeance and atonement are in the hands of God but they can be influenced by
the obedience of men.

Another observation which supports the interpretation
offered here is that the exhortation by Taxo (put forth by
the author of AM) "to die rather than to transgress the Law"
is most clearly paralleled in other examples of non-resistance,
in the death of the mother and her seven sons in 2 Maccabees
7:2, and in the exhortation to obedience in the face of torture and death in 4 Maccabees 9:1, where the holy war is seen
as an internal struggle against the temptations of Satan.
The closest parallel, however, is that recorded by Josephus
regarding the Jews who bared their throats to Pilate's henchmen (A.D. 26-36) as a protest against his illegal introduction of standards into Jerusalem. He writes that they exclaimed they "were ready rather to die than to transgress
the law." (War 2:174). Compare also Josephus' account of
the Jews who protested to Petronius regarding Gaius' attempt
to place a statue in the temple (A.D. 40). They said "that
if he wished to set up these statues he must first sacrifice
the entire Jewish nation: and that they presented themselves,
their wives and their children, ready for slaughter." (War
2:197). Both these last examples occurred (A.D. 26-40) near
the time span of the writing of AM. Both actions of passive
resistance succeeded in reversing impious activity on the part
of the Romans.

It may be that the program of passive resistance put
forth by the author of AM was simply illustrative of this
period in Jewish history (4 B.C. - A.D. 48). The War of Varus

---

[12] J. Licht, "Taxo, or the Apocalyptic Doctrine of
Vengeance," JJSt. 12 (1961), 95-103.

in 4 B.C. crushed numerous revolts throughout Palestine. Such a conquest (as it is referred to in AM) may have destroyed the revolutionary leaders and their followers and resulted in a suppression of the revolutionary spirit of the vanquished Jews. The revolt of Judas in A.D. 6 may have been much less significant than it is often portrayed,[13] and its failure simply may have reinforced the Jewish sense of futility regarding the use of arms. The recent suppression of revolution may have resulted in a resurgence of apocalyptic faith in God's (as contrasted with man's) action against the enemy. It also seemed to result in a search for alternative ways of dealing with the oppressive foreign power, Rome. But this, it is to be recognized, is conjectural.[14]

While there is little evidence of revolutionary activity in this period, there are examples of passive resistance --in the time of Pilate and again with the reaction to the attempt to place a statue of Gaius in the temple. In this period, the author of the Assumption of Moses exhorted obedient death as a way to guarantee vengeance against the enemy. Likewise, the sect of Qumran provided as an alternative the withdrawal to the wilderness of the Dead Sea to carry out an atoning obedience to the law. And it is possible to date 4 Maccabees, which may also be a passivist tract, in this same period. This period of Jewish history characterized by the predominance of non-resistance or passive resistance came to an end in A.D. 48, at which point Josephus' narrative records the first act of conspiratorial revolution since A.D. 6. With the breakdown of social and political stability in Palestine in the 50's and 60's, the revolutionary spirit again prevailed in the Jewish nation. From this point on in Josephus' history of the first century we hear no more of Jewish passive resistance against the Romans.

Such an understanding of the period from 4 B.C. to A.D. 48 may also provide a viable background for the rise of the Christian movement. The Jewish nation as a whole was grappling with what it meant to be God's people, groping for alternative non-revolutionary ways to maintain obedience to

---

[13]In the War, Josephus has only a brief notice of Judas' revolt (War 2:118). Although the account is expanded in Antiquities 18:4-10, Josephus does not even find it necessary to say that the Romans quelled the revolt. He implies that the people were dissuaded from revolt by "the arguments of the high priest Joazar" (18:3). The account of Judas' revolt in Acts 5:37 does imply that Judas was killed by the Romans and his followers scattered. But here the revolt is compared to the four hundred men who followed Theudas (Acts 5:36) and the earliest Christian movement. The only reference to the revolt which implies that it was of major dimensions is Antiquities 18:9, which claims that the populace "responded gladly" to Judas' call for independence. However, this passage is so rife with Josephus' apologetic desire to blame the later war on the instigation and innovation of Judas that it is clear the "glad response" is a telescoping of the revolutionary spirit of the 50's and 60's with the revolt of Judas in A.D. 6. Hence, there is little evidence that this revolt was as significant as it is often portrayed.

[14]However, it is partly based upon a more detailed examination of this period in my dissertation, "Some Jewish Revolutionaries in Palestine from A.D. 6 to A.D. 73 According to Josephus" (Duke University, 1973).

the law in the midst of occupation by a foreign power. The admonition to love one's enemy, the challenge to take up one's cross, the prohibition against judging so as to leave vengeance in God's hands, the active decision to obey God rather than men with an attitude of non-resistance in the face of persecution, the attempts to grapple with the atoning significance of an obedience unto death, and other aspects of the Christian movement, may all have been characteristic of the struggle of many Jews in this period of their nation's history following the War of Varus to avert a resurgence of the revolutionary spirit.

The Assumption of Moses may thus bear witness to a spirit and a milieu which pervaded the Jewish nation from 4 B.C. to A.D. 48, a spirit which predominated over the revolutionary impetus of the times and a milieu which formed the cradle of the Christian faith.

David M. Rhoads
Carthage College
Kenosha, Wisconsin

Interpreting Israel's History: The Testament of

Moses as a Rewriting of Deut 31-34

Daniel J. Harrington

During the past few years the understanding of history in the Testament of Moses has been the subject of several independent investigations which have produced contradictory conclusions. By the term "understanding of history" I mean that interpretative scheme placed on the past, present and future; in other words, the author's evaluation of the "facts" of history. In determining the understanding of history in any document one must examine the emphases, the divisions, the eschatological expectations, and the self-understandings expressed.

Klaus Haacker sees in TM the Samaritan understanding of history, according to which (1) the time of grace includes the kingdom of Joshua and his successors through Samson, and (2) the time of divine displeasure begins with Eli and continues on. Since 8.1 refers to Hadrian's edict against the Samaritans, TM must be a Samaritan book composed after A.D.135.[1] Enno Janssen discerns a tripartite division of Israel's history in TM. Each period is signaled by a major figure of saving significance--Moses, Ezra (so he reads 4.1) and Taxo. While the covenant relationship was not totally destroyed with the Exile, the guardians of the cult have acted in such a way as to make true worship impossible in the present time. The work is a testament composed after Herod's death by a member of some dissident Palestinian group which was opposed to the priests and scribes.[2] Finally, George Nickelsburg has discovered in TM the pattern of history found in Deut 28--30 according to which Israel's history is viewed in the framework of sin--punishment-- repentance (or, turning point)--salvation. For him the original composition antedates the Maccabaean purification of the Temple; chap. 6 which clearly alludes to Herod is an interpolation, the result of a post-Herodian updating of the earlier composition written against the threat of Antiochus Epiphanes. The book originated in the priestly wing of the Hasidic movement, and the updating was undertaken probably among the Essenes.[3]

The issues raised by these three studies are large and obviously cannot be resolved in one brief paper. But perhaps

---

[1] K. Haacker, "Assumptio Mosis--eine samaritanische Schrift," Theologische Zeitschrift 25 (1969) pp. 385-405.

[2] E. Janssen, Das Gottesvolk und seine Geschichte. For full bibliographical data and a summary of contexts, see the appendix.

[3] G.W.E. Nickelsburg, Jr., Resurrection, Immortality, and Eternal Life in Intertestamental Judaism, Harvard Theological Studies XXVI (Cambridge; Harvard, 1972), pp. 29, 43-45.

I can at least confirm or refine their conclusions by concentrating on what seems to be the main source, Deut 31--34. First of all, I intend to review the understanding of history in the biblical passage. Then, I would like to explore the understandings of history which were connected with Deut 31--34 in three representatives of what can be called the "rewritten Bible" (<u>Jubilees</u>, Pseudo-Philo and Josephus). These explorations will have then set the stage for a full-scale assessment of the understanding of history in TM. Finally, in order to place the issue of the understanding of history in a wider perspective I will add by way of an appendix a summary and brief critique of Enno Janssen's book <u>Das Gottesvolk und seine Geschichte</u>, a little noticed but potentially important work.[4]

I. Israel's History in Deut 31--34:

Since this paper has its origin in George Nickelsburg's remark that TM "is a rewriting of Deuteronomy 31--34,"[5] we will take the understanding of history in Deut 31--34 itself as the starting point here in our own investigation. By the canons of modern biblical scholarship this section is "a series of appendices of varied contents from various sources . . ."[6] Our interest here, however, is in discovering the directions and tendencies which could have inspired the author of TM to use the passage as his primary source.

The basic scene of Deut 31--34--Moses' instructions to Joshua prior to his death--is, of course, the setting of TM. In Deut 31 Moses makes arrangements for Israel's future in respect to Joshua's leadership, the public reading of the Law, and the placing of the book of the Law besides the Ark. Within this framework Moses says several things about Israel's history in the years to come after his death and its entrance into the land. Moses is the one who sees all this beforehand by divine revelation. He knows that he will die before entering the land, that Joshua will lead the people over into the land, that Israel will take possession of the land, and that Israel will play the harlot after the strange gods. The time after Moses' death, despite the fact that it is the time in which Israel takes possession of the promised land, is foreseen as the time of rebellion. Israel was rebellious during Moses' own lifetime (31:27), but it will be even more rebellious after his death. Its sin will be turning to other gods (31:16, 18, 20) and so breaking the covenant (31:16, 20). For this God will forsake Israel (31:17), and many evils and troubles will come upon it (31:17, 21, 29). The "Song of Moses" to be reproduced in Deut 32 is viewed as God's witness over against Israel when all these things come to pass (31: 19, 21): "For I know the purposes which they are already forming, before I have brought them into the land that I swore to give them (31:21)."

---

[4]See pp.

[5]Nickelsburg, p. 29.

[6]G. Henton Davies, "Deuteronomy," in <u>Peake's Commentary on the Bible</u> (London: Nelson, 1962) p. 282 (#242f).

The "Song of Moses" in Deut 32 surveys the past by
emphasizing God's goodness in creation (32:6), in choosing
Israel as his own portion (32:9), and in caring for Israel
in the wilderness (32:10-14). Yet Israel's prosperity will
lead to apostasy and a seeking after new and abominable
practices (32:15-18). Because Israel has forgotten its Rock,
God will hide his face and bring his punishments upon it
(32:19-25). Yet lest Israel's dispersion and destruction
should lead its enemies to suppose that this was their
triumph rather than God's judgment, God will finally vindicate his people. There will be no mistake about it:
vengeance and recompense is the Lord's (32:35). He will intervene and vindicate his people. In this chapter, then, we
have Yahweh's care in the past contrasted with Israel's
future sin of apostasy and its consequent punishments. The
final vindication is traced to God's goodness alone; it is
not said to be the result of Israel's repentance. In a real
sense the "Song of Moses" with its note of final vindication
expands and completes the simple apostasy--punishment scheme
of Deut 31:16-18, 20-21, 29. While the land is acknowledged
to be a divine gift, Israel's greatest prize is its covenant
relationship with Yahweh. Whatever the origins of this song,
as it now stands in Deut 32, it serves as a witness over
against Israel to be consulted and pondered when the events
described take place. As the "Song of Moses," it is a prophetic look into the future and a warning to the people of
coming generations.

The remainder of Deut 32 and Deut 33--34 have less
direct relevance to the theme of history than the earlier
parts. Elements which have some echoes in TM are the final
blessing bestowed by Moses on the tribes of Israel in
Deut 33, the death of Moses at 120 years of age and his subsequent burial in the place which "no man knows (Deut 34:6)."

In summary, Deut 31--34 with its descriptions of Moses'
instructions to Joshua on the mountain and of Moses' death
sets the scene for TM. But even more significant is that
Deut 31--32 with its efforts to interpret Israel's future
history according to the pattern of apostasy--punishment--
vindication suggests the area of concern which occupies the
author of the TM.

II. Israel's History in Three Rewritings of Deut 31--34

The scene of Jubilees 1 is ostensibly that suggested
by Exodus 24:18, yet there are indications that Moses' fortyday stay on Sinai has been joined with the events prior to
his death as described in Deut 31--34. First of all, it is
said that "God taught him the earlier and the later history
of the division of all the days of the law and of the
testimony (1.4)."[7] While the bulk of Jubilees itself is concerned with past history from Moses' standpoint, he is explicitly told in Jubilees 1 to write about events "which shall
come to pass (1.26)." In other words, Moses is instructed
to view both the past and the future history of Israel; this
is precisely the concern of Deut 31--32. Secondly, the book

---

[7]All Jubilees quotations are taken from R.H. Charles,
Apocrypha and Pseudepigrapha of the Old Testament, vol. II,
pp. 11-13.

of Moses is to function as a witness against the people of
Israel, just as the "Song of Moses" in Deut 31--32 is to do.
The idea is that future generations will be able to look into
the book and see how righteous God is and how stubborn his
people has been. Thirdly, the influence of Deut 31 is confirmed by the presence of two possible quotations from the
passage: (1) "the land flowing with milk and honey" (Deut 31:
20=Jubilees 1.7); (2) "I know their rebellion and stiff neck"
(Deut 31:27=Jubilees 1.7). These two expressions are obviously Deuteronomistic cliches, and little weight can be
placed on them. Yet their presence in Jubilees 1 does add
some force to an already strong argument that the passage
conflates Exod 24:18 and Deut 31--32. Finally, the most significant parallel of all between Jubilees 1 and Deut 31--32
seems the attempt to understand Israel's future history.
(1) When Israel is given the land, it will eat and be satisfied
and then "turn to strange gods (1.8)." (2) God will hide his
face (1.13), and Israel will be punished severly and handed
over to the Gentiles. (3) After this, the people "will turn
to me . . . and they will seek me (1.15)." (4) Finally, God
"will disclose to them abounding peace with righteousness, . . .
and they shall be for a blessing and not for a curse (1.16)."
We recognize the apostasy--punishment--vindication scheme
of Deut 32 with the important insertion of repentance. This
element of repentance is underscored in the dialogue between
God and Moses in Jubilees 1.19-26. God knows that Israel
"will not be obedient till they confess their own sin and the
sin of their fathers (1.22)." Therefore, at the very beginning of Jubilees we have a scene with powerful echoes of
Deut 31--34 or, more precisely, of Deut 31--32. In this
scene Moses is said to foresee the future history of Israel
and to have revealed to him in advance the proper interpretation of this history: apostasy--punishment--repentance--
vindication.

Deut 31--34 is also treated in Pseudo-Philo's Liber
Antiquitatum Biblicarum 19. Moses, aware that he is about to
die, knows what the future history of Israel will be: (1)
Israel will arise and forsake the Law; (2) God will forsake Israel and its enemies will have dominion; (3) God will
remember the covenant (19.2). This is obviously the
apostasy--punishment--vindication pattern of Deut 32. The
way in which Israel is to abandon the covenant is specified
as idolatry; Moses is forbidden to enter the land "lest thou
see the graven images whereby this people will be deceived
and led out of the way (19.7)."[8] The author of LAB depicts
Moses as the seer not only of future earthly history but also
of heavenly matters. He is given visions of the places from
which the world is watered, the source of the manna, the
pattern of the sanctuary and the rainbow (19.10-11). Finally,
he asks for and is given a calculation concerning the measure
of time which has passed by and which remains (19.14-15)
before the divine visitation in which he (= Moses) will be
raised from the dead (19.12-13). God himself buries Moses,
and no one knows the place of his tomb (19.12, 16).

---

[8]All Pseudo-Philo quotations are taken from M.R. James,
The Biblical Antiquities of Philo (London: SPCK, 1917),
pp. 127-132.

M.R. James[9] pointed out two possible parallels between LAB and TM. First of all, LAB 19.3 describes Moses as praying "for our sins at all times." TM 11.11 asks: "Or who shall pray for them, not omitting a single day" once Moses has departed. Also TM 11.19 pictures Moses as one "who every hour, day and night had his knees fixed to the earth, praying and looking for help to Him . . ." Since both works agree in applying the description to Moses, there is some force to the parallel. But since this kind of thing is also said of Jeremiah in other writings (2 Macc 15:14; 2 Baruch 2.2), we should probably be cautious about assuming direct relationships. The second parallel concerns the time between Moses' death and the final judgment. TM 10.11 has "two-hundred-and-fifty times" while LAB 19.15 has "two and a half." James rightly terms the parallel "superficial."[10]

Josephus in his Antiquities[11] is particularly eager to emphasize Moses' power to foresee the future. The "Song of Moses" is described as "a poem in hexameter verse . . . containing a prediction of future events, in accordance with which all has come and is coming to pass, the seer having in no whit strayed from the truth (Ant. 4.303)." He summarizes Deut 32: "Moses foretold, as revealed to him by the Divinity," that if Israel transgressed the commandments, afflictions would befall the people. But God who created Israel will restore it. Again we can sense the apostasy--punishment--vindication pattern. Then Josephus adds poignantly: "Yet will they be lost not once, but often (Ant. 4.314)." This apparent "throw-away" line suggests that the pattern of history of Deut 32 is capable of even further expansion--a process which the author of TM worked out in detail. Finally, even Deut 33 is described as prophecy: Moses "prophesised to each of the tribes the things that in fact were to come to pass . . . (Ant. 4.320)." By way of conclusion Josephus stresses that Moses wrote about his own death "for fear lest they should venture to say that by reason of his surpassing virtue he had gone back to the Deity (Ant. 4.326)."

These three representatives of the "rewritten Bible" all view Deut 31--34 as a prediction of Israel's future history. Moses is the prophet who is given a glimpse of what will befall his people. Both Pseudo-Philo and Josephus retain the apostasy--punishment--vindication scheme of Deut 31--32 while Jubilees 1 refines the pattern by inserting "repentance." Finally, Josephus indicates that the pattern is not a once-for-all series of events but has been and is now continuing on in Israel's history.

III. Israel's History in the Testament of Moses
The opening chapter of the Testament of Moses[12] utilizes the framework of Deut 31; Moses instructs Joshua and hands on his power to him. The scene is also used as a device for a look at Israel's history before Moses' death. Moses' passing is said to take place two thousand and five hundred years after the creation of the world (1.2). The world has been

---

[9] James, pp. 127, 131.

[10] James, p. 131.

[11] All Josephus quotations are taken from the Loeb series, vol. IV, pp. 621-635.

[12] All Testament of Moses quotations are taken from R.H. Charles, Apocrypha and Pseudepigrapha of the Old Testament, vol. II, pp. 414-424.

created because of Israel, but this purpose has not been revealed to the Gentiles so that they might convict themselves (1.12-13). Moses was prepared before the creation of the world (it may not be proper to speak of his "pre-existence") to be the mediator of God's convenant (1.14). The Temple was made before the foundation of the world, and there the books of the Law will be preserved "in the place which He made from the beginning of the creation of the world (1.17)." Now Israel is about to enter the land given to its fathers.(1.8).

In TM 2.1--10.10 we hear Moses explaining to Joshua his vision of Israel's future history. When Joshua leads Israel into the land and organizes the kingdom, everything will be pleasing to the Lord. After the period of the Judges and the first three kings, the ten tribes of Israel will become apostates. The two tribes will continue to offer sacrifices to God in his Temple at Jerusalem during the reigns of twenty kings of Judah. Seven of these kings will advance the strength and prosperity of Judah; nine will enjoy the divine protection; four will transgress the covenant. Their basic sin is <u>APOSTASY</u> manifested in idolatry: "And they shall sacrifice their sons to strange gods, and they shall set up idols in the sanctuary, to worship them (2.8)."

Because of Israel's apostasy a king from the east (Nebuchadnezzar) will come to conquer the land and to take captive the remaining two tribes. When in exile, all the tribes will cry to heaven and ask God to remember his covenant (3.9). They also will recall that Moses foresaw all these events: "Behold these things have befallen us after his death according to his declaration . . . .(3.13)"--an allusion to the function of the "Song of Moses" according to Deut 31:19, 21. So in chap. 3 of TM exile is viewed as <u>PUNISHMENT</u> for apostasy.

Through the intercession of one who is <u>supra eos</u> (4.1 most likely refers to Daniel, but Ezra is a possibility) God remembers his covenant and shows his compassion by allowing Israel to return to its land. But this can be described only as <u>PARTIAL VINDICATION</u>, for the two tribes "will not be able to offer sacrifices to the Lord of their fathers (4.8)." Then will come another time of chastisement and vengeance because of those "slaves, sons of slaves (5.4)" who purport to be priests. These will pollute the house of worship and will go "a-whoring after strange gods (5.3)." They will favor the the rich, take bribes and pervert justice (5.5). On account of them Israel shall be filled with lawless deeds and iniquities (5.6)." Once more Israel's fundamental sin is <u>APOSTASY</u>.

Chapter 6 obviously refers to Herod, and chap. 7 may continue either the description of the pre-Maccabaean Hellenizing priests of chap. 5 or that of some group in Herod's time. At any rate, chap. 6, since it precedes the section about Antiochus Epiphanes, is out of place; chap. 7 really does not add any significant step to the scheme.

As <u>PUNISHMENT</u> God will stir up Antiochus Epiphanes (8.1) who will make Israel's apostasy even worse by forbidding circumcision, by establishing the cult of Venus and by forcing Israelites to blaspheme the name of God in his holy Temple (8.2-5). But Taxo from the tribe of Levi assures his seven sons of God's <u>ESCHATOLOGICAL VINDICATION</u>. Because they and their ancestors have not tempted God or transgressed

the commandments (9.46) they represent some kind of faithful
remnant. They foresee that if they remain faithful to the
Law, their martyrs' blood will be avenged by God. TM 10.1-10
then serves as Taxo's hymn of eschatological vindication:
the power of Satan will be broken; Israel's guardian angel
will avenge it from its enemies; accompanied by signs and
portents, God will arise to punish the Gentiles and destroy
their idols; finally, Israel will be exalted to eternal
blessedness in heaven. It is worth observing here that Israel's
blessed state is described in 10.8 in terms taken from Deut
33.29.

After this look into Israel's future Moses tells Joshua
that before God arises for judgment there will be "two-hundred
and fifty times." Joshua, knowing what is about to happen,
protests that no single place deserves to be the site of
Moses's grave (11.5-8) and that he cannot succeed Moses in
feeding, guiding and praying for the people. Moses assures
Joshua that God, who has created all nations, has foreseen all
that will happen. Out of his compassion and long suffering
God has appointed Moses to pray for Israel's sins and to make
intercession for them (12.6-7). Those who fulfill the commandments will increase while those who do not will be punished
(12.10-11).

Conclusions
How then does TM understand Israel's history? The most
significant emphasis in the work is on the purity of Israel's
cult; Israel's apostasy is concretized by its failures in
respect to the Temple and its sacrifices. The return from
the Babylonian captivity is only a partial vindication because
the restored cult is in the hands of improper priests.
History is seen in all its breadth from creation to Israel's
exaltation to heavenly blessedness at the end of time. What
is stressed is God's foreknowledge of the whole sweep. Moses
and the Temple were prepared before creation. Israel's history
from the entrance into the land represents a modification of
the Deut 31--32 pattern: APOSTASY, PUNISHMENT, PARTIAL
VINDICATION, APOSTASY, PUNISHMENT, ESCHATOLOGICAL VINDICATION.
Note that REPENTANCE does not seem to be part of this scheme
as it so clearly is in Jubilees 1. Israel's vindication in
TM is not obtained on account of its own merits or its own
efforts. Another important departure from the simple pattern
of Deut 31--32 is the presence in TM of significant intercessors such as Moses, Daniel (Ezra?) and Taxo. Particularly
in respect to Taxo, Nickelsburg is correct in seeing a close
parallel with 2 Macc 7 (the martyrdom of the seven brothers and
their mother)[13] but I do not think this significant intercession need by equated with the item of repentance.

The Testament of Moses is clearly a rewriting of Deut
31--34. The scene--Moses' final instructions to Joshua--is
the same. There are several direct quotations which undergird

---

[13]Nickelsburg, pp. 93-111. N has suggested to me (by
letter) that 2 Macc 3 ff may represent the historicizing of
the apocalyptic scheme in TM with the difference that 2 Macc
was composed after Judas and must necessarily shape the
future expectations to fit the facts of history. I have not
had time to explore this very intriguing suggestion.

the whole structure: e.g. TM 1.6= Deut 31:7; 1.8, 10 = 31:7
1.15 = 31:16; 1.16 = cf. 31:9ff; 2.1 = 31:7; 3.12 = 31:28;
10.8 = 33:29; 10.14 = 31:7. Finally and most importantly
the pattern which the <u>Testament of Moses</u> discerns in history
is a variation in the light of pre-Maccabean history and
eschatological expectation of the APOSTASY--PUNISHMENT--
VINDICATION scheme of Deut 31--34. I do not see any need to
appeal to Deut 28--30 as a source for the scheme of history
in the <u>Testament of Moses</u>. I do not find the step of
REPENTANCE which Nickelsburg traces to Deut 30:2[14] really
present in this work. I admit that the step is present in
<u>Jubilees</u> 1, but in the <u>Testament of Moses</u> it is the inter-
cession of Moses, Daniel (?) and Taxo which sparks Israel's
vindication. I think that the pattern suggested by Deut 32
is sufficient to explain the interpretative scheme of the
<u>Testament of Moses</u>.

I hesitate to present form-critical conclusions on such
a narrow base as I have built in the paper, but I will at
least offer "some observations." Among other things (besides
being a testament and an apocalypse?) the <u>Testament of Moses</u>
is a "rewriting" of Deut 31--34. The <u>Sitz im Leben</u> in the
Antiochian persecution which Nickelsburg has worked out seems
very convincing to me. So in the priestly wing of the early
Hasidic movement we have an author who feels impelled to in-
troduce precisions into the simple pattern of history found
in Deut 32. He cannot believe that the return from Exile
constituted the final vindication. In view of the enormities
brought about under Antiochus Epiphanes he reinterprets that
scheme and projects the final vindication onto the "day of the
Lord." The use of Deut 31--34 in <u>Jubilees</u> 1, <u>Pseudo-Philo 19</u>,
Josephus and the <u>Testament of Moses</u> shows that this passage
was considered an apt vehicle for describing Israel's "future
history"--a tendency already present in the biblical passage.
This observation raises an important (but probably unanswerable)
question. Was the <u>Testament of Moses</u> written in the way it
was because testaments tend to be predictions of the future,
or because Deut 31--34 leaves itself open to interpretation as
a prediction of the future? In other words, was the author try-
ing consciously to produce a testament or an apocalypse, or was
his more fundamental aim to revise and rewrite Deut 31--34 for
his own situation? This paper has supplied enough information
to make the latter a real possibility.

Appendix: Israel's History in Other Works

<u>Summary and Critique of Enno Janssen, Das Gottesvolk und seine
Geschichte. Geschichtsbild und Selbstverständnis im
palästinensischen Schrifttum von Jesus Sirach bis Jehuda
ha-Nasi</u> (Neukirchen-Vluyn: Neukirchener, 1971), 212 pp.

Taking as his starting point D. Rössler's contention
expressed in <u>Gesetz und Geschichte</u> (1962) that only apocalyptic
circles in post-biblical Judaism developed a real notion of
history, Enno Janssen, who has been a pastor in Lübeck since
1961 and holds a teaching position in Jewish studies at
Hamburg, aims to analyze what history meant for various
Palestinian Jewish writers between 200 B.C. and A.D. 200. Far
from being a collection of episodes, the "praise of famous men"
in <u>Ben Sira</u> 44-50 views Israel's history as a continuous and
unbroken chain through which wisdom and the knowledge of God
have been transmitted. Israel's wisdom and obedience toward

---

[14]Nickelsburg, p. 29.

the Law, the promises made to its prophets and its eschatological hopes find fulfillment in the high priest Simon (chap. 50). The Temple cult where wisdom (=the Law) dwells (24:10) has significance for all the world, and the priestly dynasty of Simon and his successors guarantees the continuing existence and peace of God's people. 1 Maccabees is a theological history which is especially interested in the land of Israel and its purification. Using OT motifs (holy war, the traditional enemies, etc), the author of 1 Macc sees salvation as present through the efforts of the Maccabees and envisions a future in which this blessed state will continue as long as the line continues. In the major apocalyptic writings (Daniel, 1 Enoch, Apocalypse of Abraham, 4 Ezra and 2 Baruch) the destruction of the Temple in 587 is the great turning-point of history. While previously God had given Israel his gifts and his protection, now Israel is under the domination of the "four kingdoms"—a condition which is partly punishment for Israel's lack of fidelity, partly a necessary condition for salvation. In the eschaton God's promises to Abraham, Moses and David will be fulfilled. The Testament of Moses, composed after Herod's death by a member of some dissident Palestinian group opposed to the priests and scribes, divides Israel's history into three major periods, each of which is signaled by a figure of saving significance—Moses, Ezra and Taxo. While the covenant relationship has not been destroyed by the Exile, the behavior of those charged with the cult have made true worship impossible in the present time. According to the Damascus Document the eras of the patriarchs and of the community of the new covenant are the only periods in which forgiveness of sins along with obedience and zeal for the Law prevail. Apart from these times, there has been only apostasy, disobedience and guilt. Unlike Ben Sira, this author sees no unbroken chain of wisdom and obedience to the Law. After 390 years of exile and punishment, the community makes an absolutely new beginning; the patriarchs are its types, and the OT prophecies its guides.

While Yoḥanan ben Zakkai sees the time after the destruction of the Temple in A.D. 70 as an interim period and while he hopes that the Temple will be rebuilt, he maintains that the atonement wrought formerly by the Temple service can be won by "deeds of lovingkindness". Where the Deuteronomist called for repentance and the apocalypticist for vigilance, Yoḥanan calls for action and study. For Eliezer ben Hyrcanus the time of Moses is the center of history, the only time which is significant for the later history of Israel. The gifts and prodigies of that time will return in the end-time. After the day of Gog, the woes of the Messiah and the day of judgment, the time of salvation will begin with Israel's repentance and will consist of the time of the Messiah and the perfection of salvation. Joshua ben Ḥananiah views history as basically rectilinear; there are no "golden ages." Periods of distress are followed by divine rescue. The messianic time will last 2,000 years; redemption is a "this worldly" event as was the redemption from Egyptian bondage.

In Bar Kocheba's revolt Akiba saw Israel on the brink of a new salvation which is intimately connected with God's gift of the land. Suffering should be borne with joy, for it is the guarantee of the coming liberation. For Rabbi Meir the time before 587 B.C. is characterized especially by the Temple and its cult while the present (the time of the "four kingdoms") is marked by the land and the Law. He who dwells in the land of Israel and observes the Law is a "son of the world to come." Simon bar Yoḥai trusts in God's gifts (land, Law and world to come) and sees the present as a time of chastisement. If Israel repents and observes the Law, the Persians will be able to break the power of Rome over Israel. The Temple is the center of the people, indeed of the whole world, for Judah the Prince. History is the great proof of God's fidelity toward his people; Rome will fall soon. After the days of the Messiah the "age to come" will be present.

The basic thesis that in Judaism between 200 B.C. and A.D. 200 there were various understandings of history has been proved. Among the particularly strong points in J's work are the method for determining the notion of history in any writing, the wide range of materials chosen for study, the limited focus that the theme of "history" provides, and the careful literary analysis of significant passages. In a book of such wide scope anyone can find statements to which he takes exception. For example, the interpretation of Pseudo-Philo as a work of Zealot tendency, the use of the term "eschatological" in connection with Sir 50, the view that 1 Macc deliberately downplays the priesthood, the contention that the Testament of Moses 4.1 refers to Ezra rather than Daniel, the dating of the Testament of Moses after Herod's death (rather than seeing chap.6-7 as a Herodian updating of an earlier work), and the slight tendency to overinterpret enigmatic rabbinic sayings all strike me as questionable. Yet these debatable points do not detract substantially from the general usefulness of J's work.

                                          Daniel J. Harrington
                                          Weston College
                                          Cambridge, Massachusetts

SUMMARY

Günther Reese, "Die Geschichtsdarstellung der sog. Assumptio Mosis (AssMos 2-10)," which is the third chapter (pp. 89-124) of Die Geschichte Israels in der Auffassung des frühen Judentums: Eine Untersuchung der Tiervision und der Zehnwochenapokalypse des äthiopischen Henochbuches, der Geschichtsdarstellung der Assumptio Mosis und der des 4Esrabuches (Dissertation Heidelberg, 1967), iii and 169 pp.

The Assumption of Moses was composed in the first third of the first century A.D. It is not a literary unit but consists of two major parts: (1) the description of history in 1:1-5,16-18; 2:3-10:13; 11:1a; (2) the narrative frame which portrays Joshua as Moses' successor in 1:6-15; 10:14; 11:1b-12:13; 2:1-2 can conceivably be placed in either part. The many themes shared by the two sections (covenant, the people of God, the prayer of petition, Moses as mediator, God's mercy) suggest that the frame and the main section are closely related theologically; they seem to come from the kind of circle which later produced Pseudo-Philo's Liber Antiquitatum Biblicarum.

Next there is a detailed exposition of the main section. In 2:1-9 the themes of the conquest, the division of the kingdom, and the failings of the kings are set in the Deuteronomic pattern of history; Israel has lost its independence as a nation because through its kings it has broken the covenant.

In the events surrounding the Exile in 3:1-4:6 theological considerations are more important than historical-political matters. Then all the differences between Judah and Israel became irrelevant; the people found its unity again and the possibility of a new beginning by recognizing that it (not God) had been unfaithful to the covenant.

The time after the Exile is divided into a period of sadness and lamentation before the rebuilding of the temple (4:8), a period when everything flourished (4:9a) and a period of apostasy (4:9b).

Then follows a time of chastisement under the Ptolemies and Seleucids (5:1-2) and the dark and harmful reigns of the illegitimate high priests Jason and Menelaus, Herod and Varus (5:3-6:9).

In chapters 7-10 the author stands at the border between history and eschatology. Not belonging to any party but perceiving himself as a member of the people of God, he resents those (the Sanhedrin?) who try to control his life and who are in fact hypocrites (7:1-10).

The eschatological tyrant will arise to punish the whole people (8:1-5). While the tyrant is portrayed in terms reminiscent of Antiochus Epiphanes, there is no need to identify him with Antiochus or to rearrange the chapters of the work.

Soon there will arise Taxo (an eschatological figure and not a historical person!) who in the midst of the tribulations of the end-time will give the signal for a festive departure to the wilderness (9:6) where Israel will experience the revelation of God's kingdom. Taxo's activity is a typological actualization of Deut 32:10 ("He found him in a desert land," etc.).

The hymn in 10:1-10 reaches its climax in the description of Israel's fate when the kingdom of God appears (10:8-10). Obviously based on Deut 33:29, this climax also contains allusions to Deut 32:13 ("mount upon the necks") and 32:11 ("wings of eagles"). When we recognize the combination of these last two allusions with the one to Deut 32:10 in 9:6, then we grasp the author's point: future expectation is anchored in God's care for Israel in the past.

The Assumption of Moses emphasizes the events surrounding the Exile because these events demonstrate God's mercy and covenant-loyalty and because they encourage the people to repent and return to God. The implication is that these events can be repeated in the near future. Israel's past and future history has been placed in the Moses-Joshua framework because Israel is now "beyond the Jordan": "What will become of this people?" (11:19). As Israel once before reached its goal of the promised land, so now God will reveal his kingdom and save Israel (ch 12). The covenant is the center of the author's theology: it is because of God's covenant with the fathers that Israel has a future. The Assumption of Moses is not only a representative of the Deuteronomic idea of history but is rooted in a kind of deutero-Deuteronomic theology. Reese concludes by citing with approval R.H. Charles' description of the author as "a Pharisee of a fast-disappearing type, recalling in all respects the Chasid of the early Maccabean times, and upholding the old traditions of quietude and resignation."

Daniel J. Harrington

THE ASSUMPTION OF MOSES AS A TESTAMENT

Anitra Bingham Kolenkow

This paper will speak to two major points -- a.) why the Assumption of Moses (hereafter TM) may be categorized under the form "testament" and b.) how its author uses such a "testament" to argue both against defeatist views of ordained Gentile power and for the possibility of intercession to bring final Israelite victory.

I. THE TERM "TESTAMENT" AS A LIMITING DESCRIPTION FOR THE REVELATION GIVEN IN TM

Both Charles and Laperrousaz defined as a "testament" the work commonly known as the Assumption of Moses. They, however, barely discuss the characteristics which put TM among those works called "testaments".[1] The alternative term for TM, "apocalypse", provides a useful counterpoint to help distinguish the value of the term "testament" as applied to TM. The term "apocalypse" (or revelation) is a general term for an event which may take place several times in the life of a person. In the life of Moses, for example, there are three times when he is said to have received and given revelation from heaven (the time of his original call, the time of Sinai and the time of his death).[2]

As both Philo and the rabbis talk about great men (and especially Moses) these great men have received a number of revelations. The most important is that which such great men receive from God (and give to their successors) on their death bed. The rabbis explain the occurrence of "revelations just before death" thus, "In order to allow the righteous to die in peace, he is allowed to have disclosures of the other world during life" (Gen r.62). Philo sees Moses' death as that time when Moses no longer speaks "general truths" but prophesies particular points to various tribes (VM 2:288). For Philo, the death-bed prophecies are those which make Moses not just a philosopher, but a prophet of the future. Thus the word "apocalypse", when given to a last-words forecast of the future, is too general. It is important that the revelation be noted as given on the death bed (the death bed reinforcing and connoting the final revelation). The word "testament" is a more definitive word than "apocalypse". In TM itself, particular emphasis is laid on Moses' death date (1:1, cf. 1:15-16, 10:12,14) as the time of his revelation. Further, as will be noted below, the point of Moses' death is important for the argument of the author and his opponents. Thus the prophecy given in this work is, and should usefully be classified as, a "testament", not an apocalypse.

II. THE BLESSING TESTAMENT

One terminological difficulty with the definition of TM as a "testament" is that the term "testament" often has been limited to works with an ethical-paraenetic intent. However, in an earlier paper, this writer discussed the Assumption of Moses as one of that group of Hellenistic blessing-testaments which forecast the future (the title being taken from the labeling "blessing" given to forecasts of the future in Gen. 27:27, I En. 1:1). These may be defined as last words giving an extensive forecast of the future (usually a history of Israel from the supposed author's time to, and emphasizing, the blessed endtime). The works often end with a description of the advantage of being a part of Israel or of the righteous. (The purpose of the works would seem to be an urging to remain a part of Israel.) The forecast of history is generally given heavenly validation either by statements that God foreknew or planned history or by statements that the knowledge came from heavenly books or trips to heaven.[3]

TM uses the common features of "blessing" testament: departure scene (1:1-9, cf. 10:12-14), and revelation of history up to the endtime (2:1-10-10). It also has a response, by the person to whom the testament is being given, to the declaration of departure (cf. II Bar. 44:1-46:6[4]). The work ends with

an affirmation of the future of Israel -- even of the unrighteous (12:9-13).
The testament emphasizes God's ordering of history from the time of creation
(1:13, 12:4,5). The author of TM, however, enlarges the common argument and
structure of testament history. Testament is made a place to argue God's
attempt to deceive the Gentiles (and thus convict them) as well as to state
God's foreknowledge of history. The author also illustrates what he considers the rationale of history by an enlargement of a common structure of
testament history -- the "Doppelschema" of history. TM's "Doppelschema" (in
contrast to most "Doppelschemas" which merely enumerate good and evil events)
speaks of the event which causes the reversals of history: good times occur
because of intercession by the righteous. TM's uses of additions to normative "blessing" testament argument and structure will be the subject of the
final sections of this paper.

III. THE USE OF A TESTAMENT TO ARGUE THAT GOD HAS DECEIVED THE GENTILES

TM has more than a common concern about the role of the Gentiles in
history. When pseudepigraphic testaments give forecasts of the future, they
generally speak of God's ordering of history (cf. II Bar. 21:5, 56:2) or
have a heavenly validation for their account of history. TM not only notes
God's foreknowledge of history (1:13, 12:4,5), but explicitly mentions God's
creation and foresight (even to the least thing) of the history, both of the
nations and of Israel. It is also not uncommon for contemporary works to
speak of God's creation of the world for Israel (IV Ez. 6:55,59, II Bar. 15:7,
21:24). TM not only argues God's creation of the world for Israel, but God's
purposeful lack of revelation of this fact to the rest of the world -- so
that the Gentiles may be self convicted (1:13). The point of Gentile knowledge and conviction is dropped[5] and left unexplained until (it may be gathered from) Joshua's response to the testamental history and Moses' announced
departure (11:1ff). The points of Gentile knowledge and action are added to
a typical response to a declaration of death or departure, where the successor mourns his own lack of competence (cf. II Bar. 46:1).

What the Gentiles do know is represented by Joshua's analysis of the
thoughts of the King of the Amorites. Moses is a "sacred spirit"[6] among the
Jews, "worthy of the Lord," "God's chief prophet throughout the earth, the
most perfect teacher in the whole world" (11:16). With Moses' death (Joshua
argues), such people would feel free to attack the people of Israel. The
Gentiles believe that without Moses' intercession to remind God of the covenant, Israel has no advocate or recourse after impious deeds (11:16-18).

Joshua's presentation of Gentile beliefs in 11:16-18 and Moses' speeches to Joshua (1:10-18, 12:1-13) show what was meant in 1:13 by the saying
that the Gentiles would convict themselves. Gentile knowledge is enough to
enable them to convict themselves in the endtime but not enough to enable
them to know what they should do when Moses is dead. Joshua says the
Gentiles know that God is for the Jews when Moses intercedes for them; the
Gentiles do not dare to fight the Jews at that time. The Gentiles thus recognize the force of the argument that what God is for, they (the Gentiles)
had better not fight. What they do not know, however, is the relationship of
God to Israel after Moses' death. Therefore, they will attack her. Moses
reveals that God always has been and will always be concerned for Israel.
God's concern for Israel is not limited to Moses' time on earth. God's forethought at creation and his creation of the world for Israel show his feeling
for Israel. This concern will not end at Moses' death.[7] Thus the Gentiles
are wrong when they think they can attack Israel with impunity -- as they
would recognize themselves if they knew God's continuing concern for Israel.
They rightly recognize that one may not act against God, but they wrongly
assume that God will be opposed to Israel always. The Gentiles assume their
writ of "allowed action" when Israel is in a state of sin. They act under
this assumption and on their own understanding they would be convictable.[8]

From the above exposition, it might seem that the Gentile misapprehension was a chance event -- the result of insufficient knowledge. TM argues that it was not chance, but intention. TM strengthens the common testament emphasis on God's forethought. TM produces a negative predestinarianism -- carrying the Deuteronomist theory of history to its derivable limit. TM says the Gentiles are intended not to know God's continuing concern for Israel (so that they will attack Israel and be guilty in the endtime). Even the timing of Moses' present revelation is part of God's plan. God did not reveal it before the time of Moses (1:13) (and it would also seem to be among the books hidden until the time of the end, 1:18) because God's intent was to deceive and thus convict the Gentiles. The Gentiles rightly believe that Moses is God's chief prophet throughout the whole world, but they have not received his full revelation. This revelation is given only on Moses' death bed. Thus the fact that this revelation is a testament is important for the argument that the Gentiles are deceived. The Gentiles could not have received the testament given only to Moses' successor Joshua -- a testament to be hidden until the endtime (1:18). These arguments about Gentile action (power) and endtime fate provide one side of TM's purposeful enlargement of known testament commonplaces. The other and complementary side of this enlargement argues for the use of intercessory action to bring the blessed endtime.

IV. THE USE OF "DOPPELSCHEMA" HISTORY -- PATTERN GIVEN RATIONALE THROUGH INTERCESSION

As has been noted, TM suggests that the Gentiles think only Moses could be an intercessor for the Jews. TM demonstrates their mistake (as well as giving additional assurance about what will happen in the endtime) through Moses' forecast that effective intercession will occur after the fall of the first temple and again at the time of the end. To do this, the author uses a common testamental history pattern, what Baltzer calls "Doppelschema".[9] In such "Doppelschemas" of history, the events surrounding the fall of the first temple and its aftermath are shown repeated again in the endtime.[10]

"Doppelschema" history generally gives no explanation of why evil periods are succeeded by good; it merely gives the events of history. TM still gives the events of history but uses intercession as that event in history which causes God to turn again to Israel. This "turning again" produces a "good" period for Israel. In TM, intercession based on covenant promise "shows" why God turned to Israel after the fall of the temple and the exile (4:1-6). The intercession of Daniel[11] after the fall of the temple gives TM's precedent (customary in "Doppelschema" histories) for what will happen in the endtime. The author of TM, having shown how intercession caused the return of good times in the past, then apparently presents what is either an urging to intercession by the righteous or an affirmation of present intercession which is being made by the righteous[12] (9:1-7). The urging or affirmation is given by making the intercession by Taxo the event which leads into the account of the blessed endtime (10:1-10).

Following the testamental history, Joshua asks what will happen to Israel when Moses is no longer Israel's ruler or advocate in the eyes of God and the nations. Moses' answer to this point has already been given in the testamental history: when Israel sins, it will be attacked by the nations; but it will be saved by the intercession of righteous men. However, Joshua is obviously worried about his own and Israel's lacks. Moses' final answer stresses God's foresight of history and his covenant and oath with Israel. Moses, the great intercessor[13] (known as such by Israel -- cf. Deut. 9:18-20, 25-29, 10:10 -- and by the nations), stresses that it is not his (Moses') virtue which caused him to be appointed as advocate for Israel. Likewise, it is not Israel's godliness that will bring the "rooting out" of the nations (cf. Deut. 9:5); God has foreordained all things. Such a statement, of course, provides an end statement for the testamental history comparable to the introductory statement which precedes the history (1:10-18). It also gives answer to a pessimism about a sinning Israel's fate. Additionally,

Moses' answer provides encouragement for present intercessors. God appointed Moses as intercessor -- and Moses' statements about God's foresight of history as well as statements about future intercessors in the "Doppelschema" testamental history would imply that God appointed Daniel as intercessor after the fall of the temple and Taxo as intercessor for the endtime. Moses' emphasis on his own lack of virtue would serve as special encouragement to the Taxo who is spoken of in the history. Taxo is the successor of Moses and the addressée of his testament.

TM's author thus uses a "blessing" testament to argue for God's continuing favor toward Israel. Against the supposed Gentile argument that God is no longer with the Israelites TM employs a pre-creation-made intercessor Moses. Moses says that the Gentiles purposefully were deceived by God (effectively so that they could be destroyed in the end). Moses then prophesies history. This prophecy forecasts that the blessed endtime will follow the (present) great time of troubles -- just as good times succeeded evil after the fall of the temple -- in typical testamental-history "Doppelschema" style. The structure of "Doppelschema" history, however, is enlarged to argue that intercession caused the change from evil to good times in the past and that present intercession will save Israel from current evil and bring the blessed endtime. God has promised this by his oath and covenant and by the testament of his covenant-deliverer Moses.

1. R. H. Charles APOT, II, 414. E. M. Laperrousaz ("Le Testament Moïse", Semitica XIX 34, 35) cites Charles and uses the label.

2. On times and contents of Moses' view of heaven cf. A. Kolenkow, An Introduction to II Bar. 53, 56-74, Harvard thesis: 1971, 102-103.

3. The form was studied by this writer in "The Genre Testament and its Use for Forecast of the Future in Hellenistic Judaism", presented at the SBL Pseudepigrapha Seminar, 1972. To be published: JSJ, IV. On the basis of this paper, it might be argued that Moses' pre-creation origin is mentioned both as a basis for his revelation and to antedate other Jewish revelations such as those of Enoch. In many Hellenistic Jewish "blessing-testaments" (as discussed by this writer), the authority for prophecy is the revealer's trip to heaven (where he saw the judgment or read the heavenly books: T.L. 2-3, I En. 93:1, VAE 25). However, in the OT there seems to be no feeling that Moses needs such authority for his last-words' forecast. TM would resemble the OT in this. (Cf. Philo VM II, 190, "God has given to him his own power of foreknowledge.") Only incidentally does Moses mention what might be a basis for his revelation of the future (his preexistence). Preexistence would merely seem a part of an apologetic argument for God's concern and against Gentile knowledge. God had had his purpose from the beginning of the world (Moses was there and is a witness). Moses did not receive his knowledge from the Egyptians -- as argued by many Gentiles.

4. II Bar. 46:4 also has an assurance of continuation of leaders. (Cf. II Bar. 77:16.)

5. The points of Gentiles' knowledge and conviction surround but are not included in the testamental history. Does this carry any implication that they are added to a source?

6. An understanding that the holy spirit is present at the time of Moses and away from Israel later is shown in Is. 63:11ff. Neh. 9:20 says of the time of Moses, "Thou gavest thy good spirit to instruct them." Charles cites Wis. 3:5 and 7:22 in relation to TM 11:16. The Amorites know their OT! In TM the belief that God was but is no longer with Israel is put into the mouth of Israel's enemies and in contrast to the revelation of Moses. Does this mean that TM is arguing against a group of Jews who argue (from Is. 63 or some similar source) that human action is ineffective in the present state of Israel's sins? Cf. J. Licht ["Taxo and the Apocalyptic Doctrine of Vengeance" JJSt. 12 (1961), 96] who argues that TM is speaking of actions -- a dying to provoke vengeance by God (97). It should be noted that in Deut. 1:44, the Amorites are the instrument of a sinning Israel's defeat. This function is still that of the nations in TM 12:12 (cf. Deut. 8:20, 28:25,49, 29:24).

7. The history also becomes a proof of the Gentiles' wrong understanding since the history begins with an account of the going into the land and establishment of the kingdom; the Amorites were not successful in opposing Israel.

8. The understanding that the Gentiles would convict one another suggests that TM has in mind the endtime trial discussed by Nickelsburg (Resurrection, Immortality and Eternal Life in Intertestamental Judaism. Cambridge, Mass.: 1972, 58-81). The Gentiles are known to be planning to destroy Israel when they safely can (11:18). (According to the history, indeed, various kings have come and done so.) They assume that when Israel sins the nations can attack with impunity and that there will be no problem with their action. They assume that the oath does not continue (12:13). They would seem to take seriously the deuteronomic theory of the nations' role as instruments of God's justice. (Cf. also the motif of surprise after almost a court case in Wis. 5:7, 5:2, Is. 52:15.) However, by oath and covenant relationship (3:9, 4:5, cf. 9:45, 12:13), the Israelites have the possibility of calling upon God. The Israelite trump card is that the Gentiles are as (or more)

impious than Israel but have not suffered as Israel has (9:3,6,7). The
nations' conviction (1:13, cf. Wis. 4:20, Is. 52:15, 53:1-6) will be from
a group realization of what they have done. The account of the endtime in
10 shows Israel's exaltation (cf. Nickelsburg, Resurrection, 82 on II Bar.
51:10). The comments of Joshua and Moses provide juxtaposing trial motifs
for the testamental history.

9. Baltzer (Das Bundesformular², 1964, 165, 170) cites I En. 91:5,6,
T.L. 16-18 (unspecified), T.N. 4:4, T.Z. 9:9. The writer has discussed
this form further (II Bar. 53, 56-74, 44-45) and, as examples of this form,
has added VAE 29, I En. 91:12-17, II Bar. 57-74 and T.L. 17:7-18:14. In
such "Doppelschema" histories, endtime repetition of events associated with
the fall of the first temple apparently is used to "explain" why the blessed
endtime kingdom did not occur at the time of the rebuilding of Israel (or in
the time of the Maccabees) as forecast by the prophets. Nickelsburg
(Resurrection, 44) effectively notes a repetition of historical pattern when
he places the events of 2-4:9 in parentheses after the similar events of
5,8,9,10.

10. The emphasis which TM (like other such histories) places on the period
of history from the time leading up to the fall of the first temple (and to
the endtime) is shown by the shortness of the description of the time from
the time of Moses to the time shortly before the fall of the temple (2:3-7)
and the extensive description of the following "Doppelschema" times
(2:9-10:10). In this latter description (covering the time usually covered
by "Doppelschema" presentations) there are two periods of sin followed by
kingly invasion and two intercessions which lead to happy periods (evils,
king from east, repentance and intercession, compassion of God and rebuilding, 2:8-4:9; evils, king from west, evils, king from kings, intercession,
final blissful period, 5:1-10:10). 5:1-10:10 might be considered a double
period itself (cf. 6:8, 8:1) -- with no good period because there is no
intercession after 6:9. Or, using this typology, it might be argued that
chapters 6 and 7 were an addition to the original text. They may be. However in a similar "Doppelschema" based history, II Bar. 68 also uses a
single dark period encompassing several "ups and downs" in the process of
history. One notes in TM that there is an extended presentation of the
particular sins (Gentile in origin) of this period and a discussion of
history which allows one to see exactly where in history one is. Perhaps
the point is that TM's author does not wish any mistake about what point in
history is talked of -- and the best way to do this is to outline the
immediate past.

11. This is a picture also evident in Dan. 9:13-17. Dan. 9 itself uses a
type of history evident also in Neh. 9, Ps. 106 (cf. Ez. 9). Such "confessional" histories cite God's past turning to Israel (after Israel has
sinned and repented) and use this as a basis for present intercession. In
Ps. 106, the basis for God's turning in the time of Moses is explicitly
stated to be the intercession of Moses (23) and Phineas (30). Does the use
of Danielic intercession (and forecast of effective intercession in the
future which takes place in TM) show that TM has taken such intercessional
history seriously and pushed "what is requested in confessional history"
into "what is forecast to occur in testamental forecasts of the endtime"?
The difference is that one gains authority for "what one wishes for the
future" from putting the forecast speech into an authoritative mouth. Cf.
Kolenkow (II Bar. 53, 56-74, 114-116) on the use and commonplaces of such
confessional histories. Nickelsburg (Resurrection, 44) is right that the
Deuteronomistic theory of history shows a reversal of times. However, TM
would seem to find Daniel as the model intercessor.

12. Charles (The Assumption of Moses. London: 1897, 34) also recognizes
the paraenetic intent of this passage. Cf. Licht, Taxo, 101.

13. One might argue that TM's stress on Moses as creation-produced -- together with the note that he is Israel's advocate -- conflicts with the "Doppelschema's" use of two other intercessors at whose behest God turns to his people. The defective text of 12:6 does not make clear whether Moses has a continuing role as intercessor. For a study of the arguments about intercession, cf. notes in A. B. Kolenkow, "The Ascription of Romans 4:5", HTR 60 (1967), 228-30. Intercession by Moses is both considered effective in the endtime (Jub. 1:21 -- Israel will not be ensnared by sins to eternity) and not working at the Judgement (IV Ez. 7:106,115).

Anitra Bingham Kolenkow
Del Mar, California

The Text of Deuteronomy Employed in the Testament of Moses

Ralph W. Klein

Concordia Seminary

St. Louis, Mo. 63105

A survey of allusions to or citations from Deuteronomy in TM produced little positive indication of the textual tradition used by the author. The following four comments may be of help in future research.

1) 1:6 Joshua's father's name is given as <u>Nave</u> in the Latin text. This indicates that the Greek translator used the form Ναυή of the LXX, itself probably a corruption of the original transliteration: *NAYN > NAYH.

2) 1:8 <u>inducat</u>. Although cast in the 3rd masculine singular, this word seems to be based on the 2nd masculine singular form of Dt. 31:7: תבוא. The form in MT, LXX, and Targum is intransitive, so that the transitive form of TM presupposes a form תביא which is attested by the Samaritan Pentateuch, Syriac, Vulgate, and 5 medieval Hebrew manuscripts.

3) 10:8 The text recalls Dt. 33:29 and the word <u>cervices</u> presupposes the reading "necks" in LXX, Targum, Syriac, and Vulgate. These versions may indicate that the original reading במותימו, preserved in MT, may have been replaced by צואריהם or the like under the influence of Josh. 10:24. The Targum's reading, "necks of their kings," is identical to the Joshua passage.

4) According to the chronology of TM, Moses dies 2,500 years after creation. This agrees exactly with none of the following: MT = 2,708 (or 2,706), LXX = 3,859 (or 3,857), Samaritan Pentateuch = 2,794 (or 2,792), Jubilees = 2,450, Josephus 2,550 (or 2,530). In any case, the MT chronology does not seem to have become dominant by the time of TM.

ON THE NON-RELATIONSHIP OF THE TESTAMENT OF MOSES TO THE
TARGUMIM
Sheldon R. Isenberg

The pleasures of scholarship are many, but rarely do they include the pleasure of making that type of study which, after judicious consideration of the arguments and evidence offered by the giants of the past, and after a fresh review of all available materials, one may stamp "definitive" with a sigh of self-satisfaction. I have been asked by this seminar to determine whether there is any relationship between TM and the Jewish targumim. The delights of such a study are hardly enhanced by the fact that nowhere in the scholarly literature have I found the slightest suggestion that there might be such a relationship. In the annotated editions of Charles and Laperrousaz the targumim are rarely referred to for parallels.[1] Yet the question of a possible relationship ought to be raised, if only for the sake of thoroughness in the total study of TM.

If indeed "the Assumption of Moses (which we designate TM) is a rewriting of Deuteronomy 31-34",[2] the targumic versions of those biblical chapters may be similarly described. TM has been dated within a century of either side of the common era and has been determined to be of Palestinian origin. The targumim to the Pentateuch cannot be dated in so narrow a range. They are composite documents whose composition may have extended over more than half a millennium. However, we know that they contain interpretive traditions which may be dated as early as TM and, with the exception of Onkelos, they are probably of Palestinian provenance. Further, they are all of Palestinian origin.[3] Finally, TM,

---

[1] The editions of TM consulted are the following: Charles, Robert H., ed. and trans., The Assumption of Moses (London, 1897); idem, "The Assumption of Moses" in The Apocrypha and Pseudepigrapha of the Old Testament in English (Oxford, 1913), 2 vols.; Laperrousaz, E. M., Le Testament de Moïse, Semitica vol. 19 (Paris, 1970).

[2] Nickelsburg, George W. E., Jr., Resurrection, Immortality, and Eternal Life in Intertestamental Judaism, Harvard Theological Studies 26 (Cambridge, 1972), p. 29.

[3] Abbreviations of targum texts and editions used: N: Codex Neofiti, microfilm copy; O: Targum Onkelos from A. Sperber's edition, The Bible in Aramaic Based on Old Manuscripts and Printed Texts. Vol. I: The Pentateuch According to Targum Onkelos (Leiden: E.J. Brill, 1959); TJI: Targum of Pseudo-Jonathan cited from Pseudo-Jonathan (Thargum Jonathan ben Usiel zum Pentateuch). Nach der Londoner Handschrift (Brit. Mus. add. 27031) (ed. M. Ginsburger; Berlin: S. Calvary, 1903); TJII: Targum Yerushalmi from Das Fragmententhargum (Thargum jeruschalmi zum Pentateuch) (ed. M. Ginsburger; Berlin: S. Calvary, 1899). On the Palestinian origins of the targumim, see my unpublished dissertation, "Studies in the Jewish Aramaic Translations of the Pentateuch" (Harvard University, 1969) and my two related articles, "An Anti-Sadducee Polemic in the Palestinian Targum Tradition," Harvard Theological Review 63 (1970), 433-444 and "On the Jewish-Palestinian Origins of the Peshitta to the Pentateuch," Journal of Biblical Literature 90 (1971), 69-81.

extant in Latin with ambiguously related Greek fragments, is agreed to have been written originally in either Hebrew or Aramaic.[4] If the original language was indeed Aramaic, then questions of linguistic relationships could be raised. It is hardly unreasonable to consider TM and the targumim together.

The possible relationship between them may be examined on several levels. Since TM and the targumim base themselves on a Biblical text, what is characteristic of each can be discerned from their respective departures from the text into various kinds of expansions and interpretations. The first question, then, is whether there are parallels in their midrashic activities. Let us consider several passages from TM in comparison with parallel targumic treatments of the Biblical text.[5]

1)   TM 1.3 and TJI Ex. 12.40-41
    TM 1.2-3: *qui est bis millesimus et quingentesimus annus a creatura orbis terrae. Nam secus qui in oriente sunt numerus . . . mus· et·. . mus et·. . . . mus· prefectionis fynicis·*

(that is the two thousand five hundredth year from the creation of the world. But according to oriental reckoning the two thousand and seven hundredth and the four hundredth after the departure from Phoenicia.)

    MT Ex. 12.40: And the dwelling of the children of Israel which they dwelt in Egypt was four hundred and thirty years.

    in Egypt]
    LXX: +and in Canaan
    Sam: in the land of Canaan and in the land of Egypt

    TJI Ex. 12.40: And the days which the Children of Israel dwelt in Egypt were thirty periods of seven years, their sum being two hundred and ten. And the number was four hundred and thirty years from [the time when] God spoke to Abraham in the hour that he spoke with him on the fifteenth of Nisan between the divided parts to the day they left Egypt.

MT has the Children of Israel living in Egypt for four hundred and thirty years, while the Septuagint and Samaritan texts have the figure encompass not only time spent in Egypt but the time spent in Canaan as well. Charles notes that the Septuagint chronology is also supported by Jubilees, Josephus, Paul and TJI.[6] Since Gen. 15:13 records that God foretold to Abraham that the Israelites would be slaves in Egypt for four hundred years, a figure in conflict with Ex. 12.40, there is ample reason to expect confusion. Without getting into the

---

[4] On the original language of TM see Laperrousaz, pp. 16-25 and references.

[5] The following four examples are all that have been mentioned by Charles and Laperrousaz, and they do not really tell us whether they are suggesting direct connections or not.

[6] Charles, 1897 ed., ad loc.

problem of original readings in the Hebrew text, let us note only that TJI is indeed in agreement with Sam and LXX against MT in rendering Ex. 12.40. TM as reconstructed by Ceriani, followed in this instance by Charles and Lapperousaz, seems to reflect a similar interpretive tradition. But the commentators seem also to agree that 1.3 is a later scribal interpolation and not original to TM. Given that the number is not original, that it is reconstructed as four hundred rather than four hundred and thirty, and that at any rate there is not evidence that TJI is directly related to TM at this point, we need consider it no further.[7]

2) TM 1.17 and TJI Ex. 28.30

> TM 1.17: And thou shalt set these (the books) in order and anoint them with oil of cedar and put them away in earthen vessels in the place which He made from the beginning of the creation of the world.

In his note on this passage, Charles queries, "Is there any reference here to "stone of foundation," אבן שתיא, mentioned in the Targ. Jon. on Exod. xxviii. 30?"[8] The Biblical passage reads, "And you shall put the Urim and Tumim on the breastplate of judgment, and they shall be upon the heart of Aaron when he enters before the Lord. And Aaron shall bear the judgment of the Children of Israel on his heart before the Lord always." TJI expands upon this passage as follows:

> And you shall place on the breastplate of judgment the Urim which illuminate their words and reveal the hidden things of the house of Israel and the Tumim which complete their deeds before the high priest who searches out instruction in them from the Lord, for in them is engraved and made explicit the great and holy Name by which the three hundred and ten worlds were created and which was engraved and made explicit on the stone of foundation אבן שתיא with which the Lord of the world sealed the mouth of the great deep at the beginning . . . .

A glance at the discussion of the stone of foundation in Ginzberg's *Legends of the Jews* reveals the complexity of the legend and the range of sources for it.[9] Where it is mentioned explicitly, as it is not in TM, it is associated with creation and with the Temple in Jerusalem. The earliest datable reference to the stone is to be found in M. Yoma 5.2: "After the Ark was taken away a stone remained there from the time of the early Prophets, and it was called 'Shetiyah'." According to

---

[7] There may very well be an Old Palestinian reading involved here. On the implications of that possibility, see the references in n. 3 above concerning the Palestinian origins of the targumim. The only relevance for this study is that the possible relationship of TM and TJI in this passage might be through a shared variant to the MT. But even this supposition of relationship is farfetched.

[8] Charles, 1897 ed., ad loc.

[9] Louis Ginzberg, *The Legends of the Jews*, vol. 5, (Phila., 1925), pp. 15 f.

the Mishnah, then, the stone replaced the ark in the Second
Temple. Although elements of the legend can be demonstrated
to be datable as early as TM, the questions which interest us
are whether TM in this passage manifests any relationship to
the targumim and whether that relationship can be deduced from
some covert reference to the stone in TM. The first thing to
note is that one may only infer allusion to the stone and that
that reference is by no means a necessary one. Charles' note
with references demonstrating that "the place which He made
from the beginning" means Jerusalem or, perhaps more generally,
Palestine, is surely sufficient commentary. There is no hint
as to why he even mentions the stone.[10] Second, even assuming that reference is made to the stone, there is no reason
to assume further that there is some connection with TJI.
There are sufficient allusions elsewhere in the rabbinic literature to make any argument for direct dependence untenable.

3) TM 8.5

TM 8.5: And they will likewise be forced by those who
torture them to enter their inmost sanctuary, and they
will be forced by goads to blaspheme with insolence the
name (verbum), finally after these things the laws and
what they had above their altar.

Laperrousaz notes correctly that the targumic literature
employs מימרא, which would be the Aramaic rendering of verbum,
to refer to God.[11] That is all he has to say about the word.
It is not at all clear whether he is merely adding to Charles'
observations which do not mention the targumim at this point
or whether he is suggesting that there is some connection. For
our purposes, we need only observe that the use of שם and its
equivalents to designate God is so widespread from the Biblical
literature and on that there is no possibility of establishing
any connection between its use in TM and in the targumim.[12]

4) TM 10.8 and TJI Dt. 33.29

TM 8.5: *tunc felix eris tu Istrahel et ascendes supra
cervices et alas aquila*

(Then thou, O Israel, wilt be happy, and thou wilt
mount upon the necks and wings of the eagle.)

Charles, in his reconstruction of the text, omits *et
alas*, thus reading "thou wilt mount on the neck(s and wings)
of the eagle," a reading which he takes to be an allusion to
a common variant reading or interpretive rendering of Dt. 33.29:

MT: על במותימו תדרך
and you shall tread on their high places

LXX: καὶ σὺ ἐπὶ τὸν τράχηλον αὐτῶν ἐπιβήσῃ
and you shall tread on their neck

TJI: ואתון על פירקת צוורי מלכיהון תדרוך
and you shall tread on the necks of their kings

---

[10] Charles, 1897 ed., ad loc.

[11] Laperrousaz, ad loc.

[12] See particularly Lev. 24.11, 16.

Charles claims that TM's interpretive rendering of Dt. 33.29, a rendering shared by most versions, may be explained by attraction to Josh. 10.24, ". . .put your feet on the necks of these kings!" Why there should be such an attraction remains unexplained. Nor does Charles suggest any relationship among the versions or say anything about the relationship between the versions and TM. Although Josh. 10.24 seems to have little relevance to the use of Dt. 33.29, the latter passage remains of great interest. The versions' renderings of במותי in Dt. 32.13 also avoids the translation of במת as "high places" or altars. Interestingly enough, there is also significant agreement among the versions, including the targumim, on the variant reading. The non-MT reading may be explained as a theologically motivated interpretation avoiding the implication that there really are other "altars of the land" that deserve the name, but this is highly speculative and requires further investigation. What is significant here is that there may well be an Old Palestinian reading that lies behind the versions and TM.[13] The Old Palestinian text was available when TM was presumably composed, so that chronology presents no difficulty. On the other hand, during the transmission process while TM was being translated from Hebrew or Aramaic through Greek to Latin, the variant reading could easily have crept in, since both the Greek and Latin traditions have the variant. At any rate, it is obvious that no direct relationship between TM and the targumim may be claimed on the basis of this passage.

The passages I have treated are those mentioned in the literature as possible connections. A closer examination of these passages than those given in the commentaries has not produced any evidence for claiming a connection between TM and the targumim. There are two more passages not mentioned in the commentaries which deserve equal treatment, although the results will prove to be equally uninteresting.

5) TM 1.12 and the targumim to Num. 22.30
    TM 1.12: For He (the Lord) hath created the world on behalf of his people.

Charles claims that this verse expressed "the prevalent view of Judaism from the first century of the Christian era onward," citing as evidence particularly IV Ezra 6.55, 7.11 and Apoc. Baruch 14.8[14] Laperrousaz cites the claim that the world was created on behalf of Israel as one of the three central doctrines of TM.[15] It is to be noted, then, that TJI, TJII and N to Num. 22.30 share an haggadic expansion which makes the same point. The following is from TJI:

> And the ass said to Balaam, "Woe to you, Balaam, lacking in reason, for I am an unclean beast who will die in this world and will not enter the world to come and you are unable to curse me. How much more is it the case with the children of Abraham, Isaac and Jacob, for whose merits the world was created . . . .

---

[13] See references in n. 3 above. Laperrousaz, incidentally rejects the omission of *cervices et* (ad loc.).

[14] Charles, 1897 ed., ad loc.

[15] p. 82.

The other <u>targumim</u> do not differ substantially here. Charles is, of course, correct about the spread of this doctrine, a kind of cosmic ethnocentrism that has plagued most cultures at one time or another. All we may conclude is that both TM and the targumic literature witness to the same doctrine; no conclusion of direct relationship is to be drawn. There are, however, shared traditions.

6) TM 1.14

TM 1.14: Accordingly He designed and devised me (Moses) and He prepared me before the foundation of the world that I should be the mediator of His covenant.

Two claims are made in this passage, the first involving Moses' pre-existence and the second more common claim of Moses' mediating function between God and Israel. The claim of Moses' pre-existence, of his being created before the world, is, as far as I know, to be found nowhere else in Jewish literature. On the other hand, the pre-existence of Torah was undoubtedly a common enough notion which might well give birth to the motif claiming the pre-existence of its mediator as well. The <u>targumim</u> expanding on the story of the expulsion from Eden in Gen. 4 talk of the pre-existence of the Torah, Eden and Hell, but not Moses. But there is a tradition that Moses' rod was one of the ten things created "between the suns," at the dusk preceding the first sabbath. I cite the tradition as it appears in TJI to Num. 22.28:

Ten things were created after the world had been established at the coming in of the Sabbath at twilight: the manna, the well, the rod of Moses . . . .

The identical tradition is to be found in M. Avot 5.6 which adds, "Some also say: evil spirits and the sepulcher of Moses." But pre-existence is not an issue in this tradition and it does not involve Moses himself. Finally, Moses' mediatorship is a Biblical tradition and requires no further comment.

I can find no other potential literal parallels, not even by further stretching the imagination. I think that we may safely conclude that the targumic literature and TM never touched each other with any discernible results. Now we may broaden the question to see how much the <u>targumim</u> and TM inhabited the same thought-world. Since the figure of Moses and the eschatology in TM seem to be the most striking elements which are susceptible to comparison with the <u>targumim</u>, it is particularly interesting to see how both are dealt with in TM 10.4ff. and TJI to Dt. 28.15 where parallel passages from Joel are cited.

7) TM 1.4 ff. and TJI to Dt. 28.15

TM 1.4-6:
4. And the earth will tremble: to its confines will it be shaken:
   And the high mountains will be made low
   And the hills will be shaken and fall.
5. And the horns of the sun will be broken and he will be turned into darkness;
   And the moon will not give her light, and be turned wholly into blood.
   And the circle of the stars will be disturbed.
6. And the sea will retire into the abyss . . . .

TJI to Dt. 28.15 begins with an introductory expansion:

When Moses began to speak these words of reproof the
earth was shaken and the heavens moved, the sun and
moon blackened and the stars gathered in their rays,
the fathers of the world cried from their graves and
all creation was silent, and the trees did not move their
branches . . . .

As I have pointed out, the similarity of the passages is due
to both using the prophet Joel. TM quotes in part from Joel
2.31: "The suns will be turned into darkness and the moon to
blood before the great and terrible day of the Lord arrives."
TJI quotes from the similar Joel 2.10 (//3.15 ff,): "The earth
will shake before them and the heavens move, the sun and moon
will darken and the stars gather in their rays." TM not only
quotes from Joel, but also quotes in an appropriate apocalyptic
setting, using the violent imagery to refer to coming cosmic
upheavals. TJI, on the other hand, uses the same imagery to
describe the past cosmic effects of Moses' words. The impact
of Joel's words in each case could hardly be more dissimilar.

That is not to say that apocalyptic imagery and eschatological speculation are not to be found in the targumim. It
is there, particularly in haggadic expansions associated with
the blessing of Jacob in Gen. 49; the so-called "four nights"
expansion to Ex. 12.42; the prophecy of Eldad and Medad in the
targumim to Num. 11; the expansions of Balaam's prophecies,
particularly in TJI, TJII and N to Num. 24 as well as in the
targumim to Dt. 32 and Dt. 33. However, in these passages in
TM and in the targumim which seem parallel, we find that the
targumic treatment of Joel involves taking the decidedly apocalyptic language and "de-apocalypticizing." Joel's imagery
is used to glorify the past power of Moses rather than to
fantasize about the future victories of the Lord.

The eschatology of TM will be analyzed in detail by
others involved in this project, and it has been previously
analyzed in the literature. There is little that can be said
about the eschatology of the targumim in general other than
that its eschatology is within the normal range of the rabbinic literature. There is messianic speculation, references
to coming cosmic wars, etc. But each expansion in the targumim requires spearate analysis given the composite nature
of the literature. An examination of all such references has
yielded no striking parallels with the eschatology of TM. It
seems, then, that no matter how one looks at TM and the targumim, there is no way to establish any special connections.
They are indeed unrelated and the study of one contributes
nothing to the study of the other.

           Sheldon R. Isenberg
           University of Florida
           Gainesville, Florida 32601

THE FIGURE OF MOSES IN THE TESTAMENT OF MOSES

by

David L. Tiede

Luther Theological Seminary
St. Paul, Minn.

A survey of the depictions of the figure of Moses in the Hasmonaean-Herodian era reveals no more unanimity than a review of recent images of Jesus in western Christian theology. Whether attracted to the respective founder of the tradition out of disdain for the contemporary cultic hierarchy or by a need for an authority in perilous times or for a host of other reasons, each specific depiction of the Moses of the law, prophets, and writings or the Jesus of the gospels documents the way in which later generations interpret their experience by remodeling the image of the founder of their tradition. Frequently, only a fine line exists between the treatment which is offered as an apology to the cultured despisers outside of the tradition and the portrait which is directed at loyal adherents who are attempting to make their image of the founder relevant to current needs.[1] Thus each depiction must be examined carefully in terms of which aspects of the common tradition have been emphasized, exaggerated, or neglected and what such alterations may reveal about the concerns of those who made them.

In contrast to many other sources concerning Moses which are roughly contemporary with it, the TM is not primarily an idealization of Moses. No matter how Philo's Life of Moses, Artapanus' presentation of the great national hero of the Jews, or Josephus' portrait of him as the paradigm of practical virtue are to be formally classified,[2] they stand apart from the TM by their concentration on the person of Moses, his actions and utterances. To be sure, it is essential to the purposes of the TM that Moses be recognized as the pre-eminent spokesman of God's plans for world history, and thus his qualifications as a prophet are particularly significant. Nevertheless, as with Enoch in I Enoch, Baruch in II and III Baruch, Ezra in IV Ezra, or Solomon in the Testament of Solomon, what is said or revealed by the prophet Moses in the TM is of primary interest to the author. Moses' identity and history are only the backdrop for these revelations. Perhaps it could even be maintained that the author of the TM felt no particular need to authenticate or defend Moses before his audience. Moses' lofty status was not in question.

---

[1] Cf. Victor Tcherikover, "Jewish Apologetic Literature Reconsidered." Eos 48,3 (1956), pp. 169-193. M.A. Halévy, Moise dans l'histoire et dans la légende (Judaisme VI: Paris, 1927), pp. 54-55, 61. Geza Vermes, "La figure de Moise au tourant des deux testaments," Moise, l'homme de l'alliance (ed. H. Calles et al., special issue of Cahiers Sioniens; Paris, 1955), pp. 68-73.

[2] Cf. David L. Tiede, "Images of Moses in Hellenistic Judaism," The Charismatic Figure as Miracle Worker (Missoula, 1972). [SBL Dissertation Series, 1]. Pp. 101-240, especially literature cited on pp. 106-107, 146-149.

Furthermore, those qualities of Moses which are placarded before the reading audience by Artapanus, Philo, and Josephus are distinct from those that the author of the TM focuses upon. In order to make Moses into something of a legendary national hero who could rival the mighty kings and princes of any national group, Artapanus must demonstrate Moses' incredible skills as engineer (27:4), administrator loved by the masses (27:4-10), cult founder (27:2, 4, 9, 12, 16), military genius (27:4, 7-9, 11, 18-19) and undisputed master of the Egyptians in his abilities as a miracle worker (27:21-39).[3] Philo, in turn, sifts the traditions about Moses with an eye to the moral and intellectual criterion which authenticated the lawgiver of the Jews as a particular kind of "divine man" (θεῖος ἀνήρ), i.e. the perfect sage (σοφός) who was especially venerated by the Stoics (cf. Sac. 8, Post. 173, Virt. 77-79, 177-178, Mos. II, 7).[4] For his part, Josephus is intent upon presenting a somewhat more approachable image of Moses, the paradigm of practical virtue, legislator, prophet and general (cf. Antiq. 3:179-180, 317-322, 4:180-193, 296-320).

By contrast, the TM does not appear to be remodeling the image of Moses according to any contemporary non-biblical paradigms of the great man. That is, the author of the TM does not reclothe the Moses of biblical tradition in the garb of a nationalistic hero, philosopher-sage, or statesman; but by a few subtle strokes, he highlights those aspects of Moses' portrait which Jews of the Hasmonaean-Herodian era who knew the biblical writings could recognize as pertaining to the office of a prophet.

The first clue to the way in which the TM is shading the image of Moses according to the profile of the prophet is found in TM 1:5. Admittedly the verse has textual problems, but once the direct reference to Deuteronomy is deleted, it appears that this is a reference to the TM itself as Moses' "prophecy."[5] Other passages in the book demonstrate

---

[3]Cf. Eusebius, Praeparatio Evangelica IX, 27. For a critical text cf. Felix Jacoby, Die Fragmente der Griechischen Historiker, III, C, #726 (Leiden, 1964), pp. 680-686. For a Greek text with English translation, cf. Tiede, op. cit., pp. 317-324.

[4]Cf. Kurt Deissner, Das Idealbild des Stoischen Weise (Griefswald, 1930) and the review of Deissner by Karl Groos in Deutsche Literaturzeitung 51 (1930), pp. 1688-1691. R. Bultmann, "The Stoic Ideal of the Wise Man," Primitive Christianity, trans. by R.H. Fuller (New York, 1956), pp. 135-145. E. Turowski, Die Widerspiegelung des Stoischen Systems bei Philon von Alexandria (Leipzig, 1927), pp. 41-42. E. Bréhier, Les idées philosophiques et religeuses de Philon d' Alexandrie (Études de philosophie médiévale, dir. E. Gilson, VII, Paris, 1925), pp. 252-259.

[5]In his 1897 edition, The Assumption of Moses (London, 1897), p. 55, n. 5, R.H. Charles dropped verse 5 because "in a book of Hebrew origin the phrase libro Deuteronomio could not have been original." E.-M. Laperrousaz, Le Testament de Moïse (Paris, 1970: Semitica XIX), p. 114, n. 5, drops the word Deuteronomio as a translator's gloss, but regards the verse as referring the the TM itself.

that such a self-conscious and interpretative comment on the
book at hand is in character for the author (cf. TM 1:16,
10:11, 11:1), and perhaps this feature can be viewed as an
adaptation of the style of Deuteronomy, since similar explicit
references are made in that book to the text as dictated by
Moses (cf. Deut. 1:1, 29:27, 30:10, 31:9-10, 31:24-26).
If Josiah's reign was a propitious moment for the rediscovery
of the last words of Moses the lawgiver, wherein as God's
prophet he rehearsed the commands and ordinances with their
corresponding blessings and curses, the TM seems to have
been written at a moment when at least certain people were
particularly concerned about what the prophet may have said
on that occasion about the future of world history.

As a prophet, the Moses of the TM shares many traits
with his biblical predecessors, most notably his roles as
a mediator of revelation and an intercessor for Israel who
even endures suffering. When the author of the TM uses the
term "mediator" ($arbiter/\mu\epsilon\sigma\iota\tau\eta\varsigma$) for describing Moses'
role as lawgiver (1:14, 3:12), he is using a word that is not
to be found in the biblical or apocryphal accounts of Moses.[6]
To be sure, Deuteronomy portrays Moses in a number of functions
which might well be called "mediatorial," but the author of
the TM reserves the term "mediator" to allude to the biblical
image of Moses going forward on behalf of all Israel and
standing between the Lord and the people in receiving the
law (Deut. 5:5, 23-33). Furthermore, while the TM thus
reminds the reader of the traditional picture of Moses
transmitting the covenant (1:14) or commandments (3:12)
which he received from the Lord, the revelation which the
Moses of the TM is primarily occupied in passing on to
Joshua is considerably different from that of Deuteronomy.
The message which the prophet in the TM conveys is not
legislation but apocalyptic secrets.

An aspect of the profile of the biblical prophet which
is closely related to the role of "mediator" and is of special
interest to the author of the TM is the image of the prophet
as intercessor (cf. TM 11:11, 14, 17, 12:6). Certainly
intercession had been counted among the prophet's tasks from
the time of the earliest accounts of Hebrew prophets,[7]
yet the deuteronomist who stresses Moses' prophetic functions
(Deut. 18:15-22, 34:9-12) also lays considerable emphasis
upon the intercessory activity of Moses. In Deuteronomy,
Moses not only prays fervently on behalf of sinful Israel
(Deut. 9:18-20, 25-29, 10:10), but he takes Israel's guilt
upon himself to the point that he is prevented from entering
the promised land: "The Lord was angry with me also on your
account and said, 'You also shall not go in there!'" (Deut.
1:37, cf. also 3:26).[8] As von Rad observes, "Deuteronomy

---

[6]Charles, Assumption, p. 6. Cf. also A. Oepke, "$\mu\epsilon\sigma\iota\tau\eta\varsigma$,"
TDNT, ed. G. Kittel, trans. by G.W. Bromiley (Grand Rapids,
1967), vol. IV, p. 612.

[7]Cf. Gerhard von Rad, Old Testament Theology, trans. by
D.M.G. Stalker (New York, 1965), vol. II, pp. 51-53.

[8]Deut. 32:51 agrees with Numbers 20:12-13, 27:12-23 to
the effect that Moses and Aaron were also guilty of faith-
lessness in the wilderness of Zin, but Deut. 1:37 and 3:26
suggest that Moses suffered for Israel's sin, not his own.

wants to move its readers with the picture of a man who, while greatly afraid, took God's wrath upon himself, and who was to die vicariously outside of the promised land."[9]

Without becoming embroiled in the discussion of to what degree the image of Moses as a suffering prophet resulted in a theology of a prophetic figure suffering vicariously,[10] it can be demonstrated that the image of Moses as a prophetic intercessor had direct influence upon Jeremiah's view of the prophetic task (cf. Jer. 15:1), and the concept of the suffering intercessor is clearly a strong part of Jeremiah's self-image.[11] Furthermore an image of Moses as God's servant and prophet who suffers in behalf of the people may even lie behind the image of the suffering servant in II Isaiah.[12] And in the first century AD, Josephus draws attention to the image of a Moses who stands very close to God as a prophet, yet suffers in the midst of his intercession for Israel: "God and I though vilified by you will not cease our efforts on your behalf" (Antiq. 3:298, cf. also 3:5-21).

Thus it is not surprising to read in the TM 3:11, "Is not this that which Moses did then declare to us in prophecies who suffered many things in Egypt and in the Red Sea and in the wilderness during forty years."[13] The same Moses who makes intercession for Israel is the suffering prophet. Furthermore, although no reference is made to Daniel's suffering (i.e. lions' den, etc.), it should be noted that when an allusion is made to this prophet, it is his role as intercessor which stands out (TM 4:1-4)[14].

Perhaps it is even possible that the author of the TM believed that Moses' intercessory role did not end with his natural life (cf. TM 12:6).[15] As can be seen from II Macc. 15:14, there were those who believe that "Jeremiah, the prophet

---

[9]Op. cit., vol. II, p. 276.

[10]Cf. J. Jeremias, "Μωυσῆς," TDNT, ed. G. Kittel, trans. by G.W. Bromiley (Grand Rapids, 1967), vol. IV, p. 858.

[11]Cf. Herbert Schmid, Mose: Überlieferung und Geschichte (Berlin, 1968), p. 100. [Beihefte zur ZAW, 110]. W.L. Holladay, "The Background of Jeremiah's Self-Understanding," JBL 83 (1964), pp. 153-164. Cf. also Psalm 99:6-7.

[12]Cf. Jeremias, op. cit., pp. 854, 863. von Rad, op. cit., vol. II, p. 261. Hans Joachim Kraus, Worship in Israel, trans. by Geoffrey Buswell (Richmond, 1966), pp. 106-112. A. Bentzen, Messias-Moses redivivus-Menschensohn (Zürich, 1948), pp. 64-65.

[13]It is a little surprising, however, that the few references that are made to the exodus (1:4, 3:11, 6:6) are very casual, and may even be traditional formulas (cf. Charles, Assumption, p. 13, n. 11). The author is not interested in working with the exodus story.

[14]Perhaps even Taxo who predicts the apocalypse (10:1-10) is also to be seen as a "suffering prophet" since it is his vicarious suffering which will effect the end.

[15]The tattered text does not limit Moses' role to the past.

of God" who was famous for his intercessory prayers for the people and city was still active in that capacity long after his death (cf. II Baruch 2:2).[16]

The concept of Moses' appointment "before the foundation of the world" (1:14) also calls for special comment. First of all, this verse should be interpreted in the light of other statements in the document about the foundation of the world. God does not choose "to manifest this purpose of creation from the foundation of the world" (TM 1:13), the sacred vessels are to be hid "in the place which He made from the beginning of the world" (TM 1:17), and "all the nations which are in the earth God hath created as he hath us, He hath forseen them and us from the beginning of the creation of the earth unto the end of the age" (TM 12:4). The central point of all of these statements is to make an affirmation about God's comprehensive plan: "nothing has been neglected by Him even to the least thing but all things He hath forseen and caused to come forth" (12:4).

Thus the statement about Moses' pre-creation appointment is not in the first instance a comment about Moses' nature. When Philo, by contrast, speaks of Moses as being sent by God "as a loan to the earthly sphere" (Sac. 8), he is indicating something important about Moses' identity: "thus you may learn that God prizes the wise man (σοφός) as the world" (Sac. 8). But the author of the TM is primarily interested in affirming that God had already designated a mediator of his covenant before he had actually created anything. God's plan is primordial.

Nevertheless, there is also some precedent for suggesting that the prophet's appointment is not due to his own superior nature, but to God's election. Perhaps the most famous instance of this is the call of Jeremiah (Jer. 1:5): "Before I formed you in the womb, I knew you and before you were born I consecrated you; I appointed you a prophet to the nations." Then in a phrase which is reminiscent of the "E" version of the call of Moses (Exodus 3-4), Jeremiah demurs, "Ah, Lord God! Behold I do not know how to speak, for I am only a youth" (Jer. 1:6).[17]

The TM does not rehearse the Exodus account of Moses' reticence to be God's prophet, but it does refrain from interpreting Moses' pre-creation election as due to Moses' own special nature, and Moses makes the disclaimer himself: "For not for any virtue or strength of mine, but in his compassion and longsuffering was he pleased to call me" (TM 12:7). Thus even the hyperbole which is used to describe Moses' pre-eminent role in God's plan (cf. also 11:16, "sacred spirit worthy of the Lord," "manifold and incomprehensible," "lord of the word," "faithful in all things," "God's chief prophet throughout all the earth," "the most perfect teacher in the world") is not allowed to develop

---

[16]Cf. Charles, Assumption, p. 47, n. 17, p. 49, n. 6.

[17]The dependence of the Jeremiah text upon the Moses tradition is now further complicated by an apparent dependence of the TM upon the Jeremiah pattern. Cf. W.L. Holladay, op. cit. Of course, pre-natal appointment to a task is not limited to the prophets in biblical tradition.

into a full-blown doctrine of the person of Moses. In spite
of Moses' lofty calling as God's chief prophet, it is God's
nature as architect and ruler of world history that is
fundamental.

At this point it is impossible to resist the temptation
of a few arguments from silence. Such an enterprise is
always open to question, but since it appears clear that the
author of the TM had a variety of traditions about Moses
available to him, and was especially fond of the Deuteronomy
account, his apparent disregard of certain aspects of those
traditions may be significant. For example, as mentioned
in note 13 above, the TM displays little interest in the
exodus story, and as a result, the figure of Moses in the TM
stands apart from a host of depictions, both biblical and
post-biblical, which focus upon the Moses who led his people
to freedom.[18] Furthermore, apart from a brief mention of
the idea that the coming of God's kingdom will mean the end
of Satan's reign (TM 10:1-2), there is nothing of the
projected war between the "angel of the presence" and his
ally Moses against "prince Mastema" or Belial/Beliar, while
that struggle provides much of the libretto for the exodus
in Jubilees (especially chapter 48) and is also remembered
at Qumran (cf. CD 5:17-20). Again two significant elements
which are mentioned in summary statements in Deuteronomy 33
and 34 are notably absent in the TM: i.e. the reference to
Moses as the "man of God" (ἄνθρωπος θεοῦ; Deut. 33:1, cf.
also Joshua 14:6, Ezra 3:2, Psalm 90:1)[19] and the special
qualifications of a prophet like Moses which are to have
known God face to face and the performance of signs and wonders
and mighty powers and great and terrible deeds.[20]

At least by means of contrast, even the silence of the
TM in these areas may serve as a reminder that the Moses of
the TM is not feted as a great national champion who warred
aggressively against Israel's foes with divine power at his
disposal. Instead of such a heroic Moses, the TM presents
a figure who protects Israel not by his aggressive leadership
but by his purity of spirit being "worthy of the Lord" and
"faithful in all things" with "knees fixed to the earth" (cf.

---

[18]Cf. the exodus motif in II Isaiah, Micah 7:15, Hosea
2:15, 12:9, Isaiah 11:11, Jeremiah 32:20 (LXX 39:20), Ezekiel
20 and passim. Cf. the Samaritan "prophet" (Josephus, Antiq.
18:85-87), Theudas (Antiq. 20:97-98, the Egyptian prophet
(BJ 2:258-263, Antiq. 20:167-172), Jonathan of Cyrene and
his "exodus" (BJ 7:437-441). Cf. Tiede, op. cit., pp. 197-206.
Even in slighting the exodus story, however, the TM follows
the pattern of Deuteronomy consistently.

[19]Perhaps the Exodus 4:16 and 7:1 passages where Moses
plays the role of "god" should also be mentioned, but the
Deuteronomy passages merit special attention in the TM.

[20]In addition to Artapanus, Jubilees, CD, and Jospehus,
the significance of such credentials was not wasted on Ben
Sira: "And He (God) made him (Moses) as glorious as God, and
mighty in awe-inspiring deeds. By his words he brought signs
swiftly to pass, and He emboldened him in the presence of the
king" (45:2-3). Cf. also Wisdom 10:16, Sib. Or. III 252-253,
pseudo Philo's Antiquities 9:7, 10:5-6, 12:2, 19:11. Cf.
Tiede, op. cit., pp. 180-184.

TM 11:16-18). This Moses is a paradigm of piety, not a bold and courageous leader.[21]

Similarly Moses' successor Joshua inherits a peculiar role. Only passing reference is made to Joshua's part in the "inheritance" of the land (TM 2:1-12, 11:11), with no mention of a conquest. As in Numbers 11:26-30, Joshua continually refers to Moses as "my lord Moses" (cf. TM 11:4, 9 14 19), and he is identified as Moses' "minister" (משרת, TM 1:7, 10:15).[22] As in Ben Sira 46:1 where Joshua is identified as "a minister of Moses" (משרת) in the prophetical office, this office in the TM was also understood to entail Joshua becoming the "successor" (successor: διάδοχος) of Moses.[23] But this Joshua is quite unlike the "mighty man of valour" of Ben Sira 46:1. He is the successor of Moses in that he is the minister of the same covenant of which Moses was mediator.(TM 1:14, 3:12, 10:15).

But as mentioned previously, the Moses of the TM transmits a very particular kind of revelation to Joshua. To be sure, Moses is the prophet who conveys the commandments, but more importantly, Moses is the prophet who intercedes repeatedly for Israel and even suffers as that prophet.

It is also noteworthy that the primary additional exemplars of prophecy who are allowed to speak through Moses are Daniel with his intercessory prayers and Taxo with his apocalyptic predictions and sufferings (TM 4:1-4, 9:1-10:10). Like Daniel and Taxo, Moses receives and transmits much more than the tablets of stone. What Joshua dutifully transcribes is basically different from what is recorded in Deuteronomy, but corresponds more closely to Moses' knowledge of the secrets of the times as mentioned in other contemporary writings (cf. Jubilees 1:26-27, 2:1 23:32, IV Ezra 14:3-6, II Baruch 3:9, 4:7, 84:2,5, Josephus Antiq. 4:303, 320).

Thus Moses comes on stage at the beginning of the TM and will march off at the end to meet his death. The scene is familiar from the biblical accounts and little needs to be done to enhance the speaker's reputation. But the message that the great prophet utters is not one of a new exodus or of hope within the existing order. Apart from the continuing office of prayer for sinful Israel, there is no cause for fresh activity or even distress. Just as surely and quietly as Moses is preparing to die, his message pronounces the pre-determined fate of the world.

---

[21] This view is also programmatic for Taxo, TM 9-10.

[22] Cf. Charles, Assumption, p. 56, n. 7.

[23] Charles, Assumption, p. 45, n. 15, suggests that in TM 10:15, Joshua is identified as the prophet like Moses of Deut. 18:15. At least Joshua is designated to carry on and transmit Moses' prophecies.

SAMARITAN TRADITIONS ON THE DEATH OF MOSES

James D. Purvis
Boston University

The central figure in Samaritan theology is Moses. Belief in Moses as the Prophet of God constitutes one of the five essential elements of the Samaritan creed, the other four being belief in the Oneness of God, the Torah as God's Revelation, Mt. Gerizim as the chosen place of worship, and the coming of the Day of Judgment. It is impossible to appreciate Samaritan traditions relating to the life of Moses without reference to the unique position he holds in this religion. While Samaritan teaching on Moses is deeply rooted in the Israelite-Jewish tradition, more is claimed for Moses in Samaritanism than in Judaism. Indeed, in many respects the role of Moses in the Samaritan religion corresponds to the role of Muhammad in Islam and, in some respects, to Jesus in Christianity.[1] As the Samaritan community bore witness to the uniqueness of its Prophet in liturgical and theological writings, various episodes in his life were singled out as praiseworthy and embellished with aggadic elements and laudatory ascriptions. Central among these was the event of his receiving the Law on Mt. Sinai. Among the other events of his life receiving attention was his death.

The purpose of this study is to review the major extant Samaritan traditions on the death of Moses. This has not been undertaken as an exercise in historical theology, although it contains much data for the study of the doctrine of Moses in Samaritan thought. The intention of the writer has primarily been to provide a critical account of these traditions for the benefit of scholars concerned with developing a synoptic view of traditions on Moses' death for the purpose of comparative studies. Not many of these traditions are known, however, with any degree of certainty, to be early. The oldest major Samaritan source utilized is from the 4th century C.E., the Memar Marqah. It is very likely that Marqah drew upon earlier sources. It is also possible that Marqah contains interpolations from a much later time, inasmuch as the extant texts of this old writing are from the late middle ages and modern times. This must be kept in mind in any comparative uses of this material. As for the medieval sources cited here, it is evident that some of these were dependent upon earlier writings (such as Marqah). It is not clear to what extent some medieval texts may have drawn upon earlier oral or literary traditions now lost. The Arabic Book of Joshua, for example contains traditions on Moses' death which reflect traditions in Marqah, but which contain significant differences. Are these differences to be regarded simply as alterations made at a later time, reflecting later theological distinctions, or are these to be regarded as survivals of earlier oral or literary sources distinct from Marqah? The latter possibility should not be lightly dismissed. It is for this reason that a number of medieval texts receive serious consideration in this study.

---

1. For studies on the Samaritan theology of Moses, see John Macdonald, Theology of the Samaritans (Philadelphia: Westminster Press, 1964), pp. 147-214; "The Samaritan Doctrine of Moses," Scottish Journal of Theology, 13 (1960), 149-162; James Montgomery, The Samaritans, the Earliest Jewish Sect (Philadelphia: J. C. Winston, 1907), pp. 225-232.

NOTE ON THE SAMARITAN PENTATEUCH

Samaritan stories on the death of Moses are based ultimately on the biblical account of Deuteronomy 31:14-34:12 in the Samaritan recension, utilizing either the Hebrew text or the Aramaic targum. The outline provided there, including speeches of Moses prior to his death, was developed into a fuller structure evident in the basic framework in the accounts which are reviewed here (see below, "Common and Disparate Elements in the Traditions"). Three observations are to be noted in reference to the biblical account and the extra-biblical stories: (1) the storytellers appear to have stressed biblical readings differing from those of the received Jewish text, although often subtly; (2) if the Samaritans employed Jewish aggadic materials in the development of their accounts (which is not out of the question), no undigested or poorly edited references to distinctive readings of the Masoretic text are to be noted; (3) the Samaritans did not allow the existence of extra-biblical stories on Moses' death to affect the representation of the biblical text in their targum.

Two good examples of Samaritan biblical readings which were important in the development of extra-biblical accounts are Deuteronomy 32:35 (lywm nqm wšlm) and 34:10 (wl' qm ʿwd nby' byśr'l kmšh). The first of these, a reference to the Day of Vengeance and Recompense, was used to suggest that prior to his death Moses delivered prophetic utterances of eschatological significance. The second was used to underscore the uniqueness of Moses, that there would not again arise in Israel a prophet like him. It should be noted also that Mt. Nebo is consistently spelled hr nb' in the Samaritan text.[2] This reading could have been influential in the understanding that Mt. Nebo was the place where prophecy (i.e., prognostication) was given.

THE MEMAR MARQAH[3]

During the 4th century C.E. the Samaritans enjoyed political respite from oppression which resulted in an unprecedented cultural, religious, and literary flourishing. This was in many respects the golden age of Samaritanism, and the period which produced two of its greatest theologians, Marqah ben Amram and Amram Darah. Under the leadership of their hero, Baba Rabba, extensive changes took place in the Samaritan community, with the development of administrative districts of Samaritan terri-

---

2. This is pronounced nāba in the contemporary Samaritan reading of the Torah. The place Nebo (not the mountain) mentioned in Numbers 32:38, spelled nbw with the MT, is pronounced nabbu. So Z. Ben-Hayyim, The Literary and the Oral Tradition of Hebrew and Aramaic Amongst the Samaritans, vol. III, pt. I: Recitation of the Law (Jerusalem: Academy of Hebrew Language, 1961), pp. 164, 176.

3. John D. Macdonald, Memar Marqah: The Teaching of Marqah, vol. I: The Text, vol. II: The Translation (Berlin: Verlag Alfred Töpelmann, 1963). For earlier editions, see I, pp. xxii-xxvi.

tory and the development of the synagogue as the central religious institution of Samaritan life.[4] The basic parts of the Defter, the Samaritan liturgy, also came into being during this time.[5] Unfortunately, this good period in the history of the community came to an end in the late 5th and 6th centuries, under persecutions from the emperors Zeno and Justinian. It was not until the 14th century that Samaritan religious and literary life began to flourish again.

The magnum opus of the theologian Marqah was a six part Aramaic work known as the Book of Wonder (spr ply'th), or Memar Marqah. Book V of this work is devoted exclusively to the death of Moses. The following is the account it contains, given not only in its essential features, but in its details (no matter how banal), and with consideration to the sequence of events. Condensation of the story would have rendered it less prolix and more readable, but would have restricted its value for comparative uses. (Numbers in parentheses indicate the section numbers in Macdonald's text.)

(1) When God commanded Moses to ascend Mt. Nebo and die, there was great consternation among all the creatures (kl bwr'-yh) of God. These besought their Lord that death not come to Moses: the angels with whom Moses had dwelt on Mt. Sinai, the Five Books of the Torah, the Five Letters of the Name with which he was clothed on Mt. Horeb (i.e. ELOHIM), the Sea, the Fire, and the Cloud all made individual petitions. (2) After God had informed them that no petition would be granted, Moses offered supplication in weeping, not for himself but for the congregation which would become bereft without his leadership and go astray (Deuteronomy 31:29). Moses then alluded to Adam, suggesting that it was the pit which Adam had dug into which he would be cast, a theme to which he would return later. In finishing his worship and supplication, Moses instructed Joshua to bring the priests Eleazar, Ithamar, and Phinehas to him. These were brought from the Tabernacle to the Tent of Meeting, along with the whole priestly house. Phinehas and Ithamar were instructed to summon all of the congregation by blasting on trumpets. When all were assembled before him, he began to teach. Moses then addressed the "inhabitants of Machpelah," Abraham, Isaac, and Jacob. The first specific prognostication of future events in Moses' speeches prior to his death is contained in the address to Jacob: it is a prophecy of the end of the period of Favor

---

4. H. G. Kippenberg, Garizim und Synagoge: Traditionsgeschictliche Untersuchungen zur samaritanischen Religion der aramäischen Periode (Berlin: Walter de Gruyter, 1971), pp. 143-171. John Bowman has related the development of the synagogue in Samaritanism to a rift between orthodox priestly circles and heterodox Dosithean circles. See "The Importance of Samaritan Researches," in Annual of the Leeds University Oriental Society, vol. I (Leiden: E. J. Brill, 1959), especially pp. 45-50; "Pilgrimage to Mount Gerizim," in M. Avi-Yonah, et.al., Eretz-Israel, vol. VIII, L. A. Mayer Memorial Volume (Jerusalem: Israel Exploration Society, 1964), especially pp. 20-23.

5. The standard edition is contained in A. E. Cowley, The Samaritan Liturgy, 2 vols. (Oxford: Clarendon Press, 1909). Avraham Ṣadaqa, of the Samaritan community of Ḥolon, Israel, has also prepared an edition of the Defter: sdwr htplwt: hdptr, 2 vols. (Ḥolon, 1962). This text, as well as other texts privately printed by this copyist and cited in this article, may be secured from Ṣadaqa, P. O. Box 2590, Tel-Aviv, Israel.

(rhwth) and the coming of the time of the Apostasy or Disfavor (pnwth), when evil will increase and the sanctuary of God on Mt. Gerizim will be hidden away. After this, Moses addressed the congregation, indicating that he was going the way of Adam and that they should take care that they not go astray. There then follows an enigmatic statement which does not relate to any specific action in the rest of the story: hrgryzym byth d lh d thmdt ᵓsq lydh ᵓdlᵓ mwty, "To Mount Gerizim, the house of God, which I have desired, I shall go before I die." Inasmuch as Moses is later said to have seen Mt. Gerizim from the top of Mt. Nebo, this is probably what is referred to here, unless this is a poorly edited element from a source employed by Marqah which knew of a spiritual transportation of the Prophet to the Holy Mountain.

Moses then addressed Joshua in an extremely sober speech which is startling in what it affirms: the time of Disfavor will come because of Joshua, and the Rāḥûtâ will be hidden from him! This contrasts remarkably with what is said of Joshua in the Samaritan Arabic Book of Joshua, and it also contradicts traditions in the Samaritan chronicles that the Rāḥûtâ was taken away and the Fānûtâ initiated because of Eli's transgression in removing the place of worship from Gerizim to Shiloh![6] Moses went on to say that things might go better in the future if only he or Aaron or Eleazar or Phinehas would be present to supplicate, to pardon, and to make atonement. After likening Moses' coming ascent on Mt. Nebo to his previous ascent on Mt. Sinai, there follows a hymn of praise to Moses, comparing him to Jacob.[7] After several extended comments on passages from the Blessing of Moses in Deuteronomy 33, Moses offered his final words to Eleazar, Ithamar, Phinehas, Joshua, the Levites, the princes of the tribes, the judges, the teachers, and finally his two sons. His last word to Joshua, unlike the earlier word, was cordial and encouraging, suitable for the one who would lead the people into the land. The congregation wept as Moses prepared for his parting.

This ends Moses' departing words, his last testament to Israel. His final speech was one which told of the future: as he said, "In the role of prophethood I stand looking at the offspring of the generations and what comes after them and what is

---

6. See, for example, John Macdonald, The Samaritan Chronicle No. II (Berlin: Walter de Gruyter, 1969), pp. 109-118; Moses Gaster, "The Chain of Samaritan High Priests," in Gaster, Texts and Studies (London: Maggs Bros., 1925-1928), p. 494; Edward Vilmar, Abulfathi Annales Samaritani (Gotha, 1856), pp. 38-39; E. N. Adler and M. Séligsohn, "Une Nouvelle Chronique samaritaine," REJ, 44 (1902), 205-206; T. J. Juynboll, Chonicon Samaritanum, arabice conscriptum, cui titulus est Liber Josuae (Leiden, 1848), pp. 180-181. The crediting of the beginning of the Fanuta to a man from the Levites named ʿAzraz bar Faʾni in Asaṭir XI. 21 is most likely a cryptogrammic reference to Eli.

7. cf. also, Memar Marqah IV. 12, where there is a linkage between Joseph and Moses: "There is none like Joseph the king and there is none like Moses the prophet. Each of them possessed high status; Moses possessed the prophethood, Joseph possessed the Goodly Mount. There is none greater than either of them." Macdonald, Memar Marqah, II, p. 186. On Samaritan traditions concerning Joseph, see especially Kippenberg, Garizim und Synagoge, pp. 225-275. See also note 48.

prepared before them." But except for the specific reference to
the Fānûtā, his remarks were mostly of a general nature, reflecting a pessimism concerning future good in his absence. He is
not credited by Marqah with any cryptic remarks regarding specific historical events of the future, nor with any remarks of
an eschatological nature concerning the end of times and any possible role which he or the Taheb (or he as the Taheb) might fulfill.[8] Marqah's silence at this point is curious, inasmuch as he
devotes considerable attention to eschatological matters (including the Taheb) in his commentary on Deuteronomy 32:35, in IV.12.

Section Three of Book V contains the account of Moses' ascent
on Mt. Nebo, his glorification, and his death. It would not be
accurate to call this the "assumption of Moses", if by this it
were implied that the Prophet was taken up into heaven. It
would be more accurate to say that "heaven" (represented by the
Angelic Powers, the Cloud, the Fire, the Glory,etc.) came down
to the top of Mt. Nebo to glorify Moses. It is not said of him
that he ascended spiritually or bodily into the seventh heaven,
or any of the spheres of heaven (as in the Jewish Gedûlat Mōšē),
nor did he have visions of Paradise (as in Pseudo-Philo, Antiquities XIX. 10). It is clearly stated that Moses died and was
buried in a cave into which he voluntarily entered prior to his
demise. There is no specific account of the journey of his soul
after it left his body, nor is there an account of anything unusual which might have happened to his body after its interment.
The following is the account as given by Marqah: Moses ascended
Mt. Nebo accompanied by Eleazar and Phinehas (who were accorded
the honor of taking each of his hands), and preceded by Ithamar
and Joshua and the whole priestly house. At the foot of the
mountain the whole congregation saluted the Prophet, while the
three priests and Joshua kissed him farewell. All of this was
with many tears. Joshua is then said to have uttered a hymn of
nine lines, with eight of the lines beginning with the words,
"Peace be to you," and concluding with epithets of praise relating to the glory due Moses for what he had previously experienced on Mt. Sinai. The congregation made one last attempt to
induce Moses to tarry with them, but realizing this was futile
bade him farewell in a brief poem containing seven epithets common to Marqah and the liturgy (Prophet, Savior, Glorious One,
Priest of the Mysteries, Crown of the Righteous of the World,
etc.). Moses ascended the mountain, crowned with light, while
all the heavenly host convened to meet him. He would ascend a
little and look down, full of compassion upon the weeping congregation, blessing them with the blessing he pronounced at Mt.
Sinai. When he reached the summit he saw the rows of angels
there to meet him and the Cloud, into which he entered. The loss
from their sight of the great Prophet caused distress with the
congregation, which, wailing, offered up a poem of fourteen

---

8. Much of what is said on the Samaritan eschatological figure the Taheb in secondary literature on the Samaritans is derived from the 14th century hymn the Shira Yetima, by Abishaʿ
ben Phinehas. See especially A. Cowley, "The Samaritan Doctrine
of the Messiah," The Expositor, 1 (1895), pp. 161-174; Moses
Gaster, Samaritan Oral Law and Ancient Traditions, vol. I: Samaritan Eschatology (London: Search Publishing Co., 1932), pp. 221-277, and passim; John Bowman,"Early Samaritan Eschatology", JJ
St,6 (1955), 63-72. For the text of the Shira Yetima, see M.
Heidenheim, Die samaritanische Liturgie (Bibliotheca Samaritana,
II) (Leipzig: Otto Schulze, 1885), pp. 85-99. John Macdonald's
study on the Taheb (in Theology of the Samaritans, pp. 362-371)
concentrates more on the earlier 4th century texts. On the earliest literary materials, see especially Kippenberg, Garizim und
Synogoge, pp. 276-305.

lines, each beginning with the words "Far be it from you (i.e., to die)," and each concluding with an epithet of praise. This poem, like the previously noted hymn of Joshua, stresses the glory due Moses because of his previous ascent on Sinai. In contrast to the people who grieved, the Angels and the Divine Powers rejoiced greatly at the coming of Moses. There then follows an account of the glorification of Moses seven times (each) by the Waters, Heaven, the Earth, the Fire, and the Cloud - the Fire and Cloud passages being heavy with allusions to Moses' earlier experience on Sinai. While the Divine Powers were supporting him, the Glory came to greet him and the Great Lord descended in the Cloud to stand with him.[9] There then follow further allusions to Sinai, suggesting that for one who had experienced such wonders, and passed from the status of the human to that of the angels, death would be inappropriate. Nonetheless, it is stated that it is the lot of all men to die, Moses being no exception. The climax of the story is then reached: Moses stood on the top of the mountain with all the angels glorifying him; God exalted him and showed him the four quarters of the world, and revealed to him what would be after the Day of Vengeance, so that he feared not death;[10] the Great Glory embraced him and took him by the hand. Moses lifted his eyes and saw Mt. Gerizim; he saw and entered the cave of his burial; and, lying down with his face toward the Holy Mountain, God sent sleep upon him and he died without discomfort and without knowledge of his life departing (literally, npš̌h blʾ ṣʿr whwʾ lʾ ydʿ).

The account of Moses' death is followed in Marqah with a chapter of commemoration of the Prophet (V.4). This section is not without some beauty, and a number of his tributes are quite inspiring - so much so as to call into question the judgment of Montgomery that Samaritan literature in general and Marqah in particular are lacking in genius and logic.[11]

Marqah's account of Moses' death may be compared with accounts found in Jewish aggadic materials.[12] Although there are some encomia in these legends with similarities to Marqah,[13] there is

---

9. Samaritan texts, especially those of the 4th century, often employ a quasi-gnostic vocabulary. It is difficult to determine exactly to what extent gnostic thought may have influenced Samaritan theology (either orthodox or heterodox) beyond the employment of terminology. See Kippenberg, Garizim und Synagoge, pp. 328-349.

10. This scene is similar to that contained in the work of the Alexandrian poet Ezekiel concerning Moses' glorification on Mt. Sinai. There it is said that Moses was given a throne from which he could see all of the earth and from which his mind could survey all things in time; past, present, and future. Eusebius, Preparatio Evangelica IX. 29.

11. Montgomery, The Samaritans, p. 295.

12. Louis Ginzberg, The Legends of the Jews, vol. III: From the Exodus to the Death of Moses (Philadelphia: Jewish Publication Society, 1911), pp. 417-481; vol. VI: From Moses in the Wilderness to Esther (1922), containing the notes to vol. III cf. also A. S. Rappoport, Myth and Legend of Ancient Israel, vol. II (New York: KTAV Publishing House, 1966, reissue), pp. 343-362.

13. Such as are found in Legends of the Jews, vol. III, pp. 479-481, where Moses is seen as being far superior to all of God's creatures, outweighing them all in the scales, and as be-

nothing quite approaching Marqah in the magnitude of praise and glorification. Whereas in the Samaritan materials Moses accepts God's announcement of his death, and the creatures appeal to God on his behalf, in a number of Jewish traditions Moses is angered by his fate and seeks assistance for petition by God's creatures. These are represented as reluctant to appeal to God for Moses.[14] There is a similarity, however, in what is said in both Jewish sources and Marqah regarding Adam and Moses' death. In Marqah, Moses alludes in several statements to his death as being a consequence of what has come about because of Adam: his grave is the pit which Adam dug, he goes the way of Adam, his war is lost through the fruit which Adam ate, etc. (V.2). Ginzberg notes a Jewish tradition that God announced death to Moses with the word "behold," because he wanted him to understand that he was to die only because he was a descendant of Adam, upon whose sons God had pronounced death (the word "behold" being used because of its use in Genesis 3:22).[15] Ginzberg notes also other rabbinic sources expressing the view that the sin of Adam was the cause not only of Moses' death, but of others "who like him were free from sin."[16] These traditions contrast with other Jewish traditions which indicate specific ways in which Moses sinned, and was thus responsible for the fact that he was to die before the people entered Canaan.[17]

THE ASAṬIR

One of the most interesting of the Samaritan writings containing materials germane to this study is the Asaṭir. This is not an easy work to classify by type. It contains aggadic materials supplementing the biblical text (with much attention to Genesis), but it has the overall appearance of a chronicle, from Adam to the death of Moses. Although Samaritans in modern times have attributed it to Moses (perhaps not too seriously), the work is anonymous. The Samaritan Aramaic text was first published by Moses Gaster, who considered it to be a work of considerable antiquity (250-200 B.C.E.!).[18] The line of reasoning advanced by Gaster is hardly convincing. The only other major investigation of the text (primarily a philological study) has been produced by Z. Ben-Ḥayyim, who has demonstrated that the work dates from the early Moslem period of Samaritan history.[19] Although Ben-Ḥay-

---

ing called the Man of God because he was half man and half God (p. 481).

14. Ibid, vol. III, pp. 431-435.

15. Ibid., vol. III, p. 423. cf. also Rappoport, Myth and Legend, p. 344.

16. Ginzberg, Legends of the Jews, vol. VI, p. 148.

17. Ibid., vol. III, pp. 424-428.

18. The Asatir, the Samaritan Book of the "Secrets of Moses" together with the Pitron or Samaritan Commentary and the Samaritan Story of the Death of Moses (London: Royal Asiatic Society, 1927).

19. Z. Ben-Ḥayyim, spr 'styr (ᶜm trgwm wpyrwš), Tarbiz 14 (1943), 104-125; 174-190; 15 (1944), 71-87.

yim would not venture a specific date, sometime between the 9th and the 12th centuries C.E. would appear to be in order.[20] It must be kept in mind, however, that such a date (determined by Arabisms in the Aramaic text, references to Arabic place-names, Islamic terminology, and even by the title itself) is applicable to the date of the final compilation, or the final redaction of a compilation. Inasmuch as this work is a collection of aggadic materials, it is impossible to date the antiquity of all of the various materials it contains.[21]

The concluding sections of the Asaṭir (chapters XI-XII) relate to the death of Moses.[22] Neither, however, contains an account of his death. Chapter XI is, for the most part, a final testament of Moses. The last chapter contains a poetic oracle paralleling the prose material of the previous chapter. A casual reading of the first of these two parts might suggest that the testament was delivered to Joshua. This is not specifically stated. XI. 1-2 contains an account of the commissioning of Joshua, based upon Numbers 27:18-19. Between the commissioning of Joshua and the delivery of his final words, however, Moses is said to have been engaged in a number of activities: He copied out the Torah, and he ascended ṭwr ᶜbr'y to view the land of Canaan and to fix its boundaries, descending when he had finished. This ascent is based upon Deuteronomy 32:48-52, suggesting that Moses literally obeyed God's command at that time. The account of the boundaries which Moses fixed coincides roughly with data found in Numbers 34:1-12. This event should not be confused with the ascent on Mt. Nebo mentioned in Deuteronomy 34: 1-8, on the actual occasion of his death, concerning which the Asaṭir is silent. The statement of what Moses revealed prior to his death begins with XI. 18; it is not specifically stated to whom his words were given. Moses' final testament consists of a prognostication of what would occur in the course of 3,204 years. This may be said to be an eschatological address, in that it understands a duration of world history of 6,000 years, followed by an ideal age (see XI. 35-42; XII. 22-26). This would assume a date of entry into Canaan by the Asaṭir of 2,796 A.M.[23] Whether this work may be designated an apocalypse is a moot question, depending upon the criteria employed for the use

---

The Aramaic text is contained in 14, 114-125; a modern Hebrew translation and notes are found in 14, 174-190 and 15, 71-86. An introduction is provided in 14, 104-114, and an index in 15, 87. I wish to thank my former student Edward Fistel for his assistance in reading the modern Hebrew of Ben-Ḥayyim. A printed edition of the text has been published for the Samaritan community by Avraham Ṣadaqa, spr ʾsʾtyr (Tel-Aviv, 1966).

20. Ben-Ḥayyim, spr ʾstyr, 14, 107-110. cf. also Kippenberg, Garizim und Synagoge, pp. 10-12. T. H. Gaster suggests an 11th century date, in "A Samaritan Poem about Moses," in A. Berger, et.al., The Joshua Bloch Memorial Volume (New York: New York Public Library, 1960), p. 117.

21. As is admitted by Ben-Ḥayyim, spr ʾstyr, 14, 105.

22. Ben-Ḥayyim, spr ʾstyr, 14, 123-125 (Aramaic text) and 15, 79-86 (Modern Hebrew translation); Gaster, Asatir, pp. 45-53 of Aramaic-Hebrew section (text) and 298-320 (English translation); Ṣadaqa, spr ʾsʾtyr, col. 22, 1. 18-col. 26, 1. 16. The chapter divisions indicated here are employed by both Ben-Ḥayyim and Gaster; versification, for convenience, follows Gaster.

23. As specifically stated in the Fitron, a commentary on

of this term. The prognostication contains, in both the prose
and poetic materials, some elements found in Jewish and Christian apocalypses: a deterministic view of world history, divided
into distinct periods; a cryptogrammic reference to a historical
person; veiled allusions to historical personages and events;
and references to disastrous circumstances brought about by evil
men prior to the final appearance of an eschatological figure.
The materials are lacking, however, in other elements characteristic of apocalyptic writings: demonic and angelic figures do not
appear; bizarre imagery and mythological language are absent;
there is no calculation of times at which significant persons,
good or evil, will appear; etc. Most of all, the address is
lacking in imaginative style and beauty, such as might have been
accomplished through the use of hymnic elements. It is almost
as though the author had attempted to write an apocalypse, utilizing some literary model or models, and failed in his attempt.
One other possibility is that the author of the Asaṭir may have
copied this section of his work from an older Samaritan (apocalyptic) work, re-writing in a style appropriate to his midrashic
chronicle.

The prose account of the future begins with a prediction of
the coming of the Fānûtâ, the age of Divine Wrath. This is alluded to by name and is viewed as something which will occur
within several generations.[24] The prophecy contains a cryptogram.
It is said that the Fānûtâ will begin with a man from Levi whose
name will be ʿzrz br pʾny (so the texts of Gaster and Ben Ḥayyim;
Ṣadaqa's text has ʿzyz br pʾny). He will make a new sanctuary,
and cause dissension among the people. `This is clearly a reference to Eli, after the Samaritan tradition that he was the ultimate source of the division between the true Israel (the Samaritan community) and the heretical Jews. The name contains two
puns: the first a pun on the name Ezra, who was viewed by the
Samaritans as bringing to pass at a later time what Eli had established at an earlier time (a typological relationship), and
the second a pun on Fānûtâ. The history of Jewish apostasy is
then traced, with a brief allusion to Deuteronomy 33:7. Moses
forecasts the destruction of the apostate sanctuary and the overrunning of the land by a hard faced people (gwy ʿz pnym). This
would appear to be an allusion to the Chaldeans, although both
the Fitron and Ben-Ḥayyim relate this to the Arab invasion of
the 7th century C.E.[25] This is followed with an account of the

---

the Asaṭir, written originally in Arabic and translated into
Samaritan Hebrew at Gaster's request. The text was printed at
the foot of the Samaritan Aramaic text. See Gaster, Asaṭir, p.
283 (text, pp. 40-41). Other Samaritan texts give a date of 2794
A.M. for entry into Canaan. So Macdonald, Samaritan Chronicle
No. II, p. 77; Adler and Séligsohn, "Une Nouvelle Chronique samaritaine," 44, 201; R. Payne Smith, "The Samaritan Chronicle of
Abu'l Fatah," in M. Heidenheim (ed.), Deutsche Vierteljahreschrift für englisch-theologische Forschung und Kritik, vol. II
(Gotha, 1863), 313; Gaster, "Chain of Samaritan High Priests,"
p. 494.

24. Against A. D. Crown, who suggests that the Asaṭir connects the Fānûtâ with Joshua: "New Light on the Inter-Relationships of Samaritan Chronicles from Some Manuscripts in the John
Rylands Library," BJRL, 54 (1972), 310, note 2.

25. Gaster, Asaṭir, p. 289 (text, p. 45); Ben-Ḥayyim, spr
ʾstyr, 15, 83.

termination of the Fānûtâ, and of the coming of great joy and
good life. The true words of the Torah will be revealed, Luz
will be rebuilt, sinners will be transformed, the people shall
dwell on the Holy Mountain, idolatry will be abolished, etc.
The specific role of an eschatological figure who would bring
this about is not indicated, nor is there any suggestion of a
role which Moses himself might fulfill at the end of days.[26]

The poetic oracle covers in greater detail the same period
treated in the prose testament by listing a succession of princes who will arise in the future. The concluding verse infers
that from the death of Moses to the coming of the eschatological
prince there will be twenty-six princes, and that this figure
corresponds to something else indicated by the number twenty-six.
Ben-Hayyim notes that the gematria to YHWH equals twenty-six,
and notes also the tradition that there were twenty-six righteous men from Adam to Moses.[27] Several Samaritan chronicles cite
twenty-six priests from Adam to Moses, and the 19th century Aramaic Molad Mosheh of Phinehas ben Isaac notes twenty-five ancestors of Moses through whom the Light was transmitted to his
birth.[28] That the number twenty-six for the future generations
corresponds to the twenty-six earlier generations from Adam to
Moses is the most likely interpretation. A problem arises, however, from the fact that only twenty-four princes are specifically cited in the oracle - i.e., there are twenty-four lines beginning with the phrase "a prince shall arise" (q‘m qdqd). Either two princes have been lost from the poem, or the concluding
verse was a later (and inaccurate) addition to the text. That
the latter possibility is correct is strongly suggested by the
fact that the second to the last verse contains a blessing which
would have been an appropriate original ending to the poem.[28a]

It is a difficult if not impossible task to identify the future princes with specific historical persons. Gaster made no
attempt to do so, and aside from several passages which he regarded as references to the Ishmaelites, Ben-Hayyim limited his
remarks to philological comments. It is tempting, however, to
identify the fifteenth prince with John Hyrcanus. This prince,
it is said, will destroy the Temple of Shechem by fire (the
text reads ’yklh, a term which is not otherwise used by the Samaritans for their ancient sanctuary).[29] The only prince who may
be clearly identified, however, is the last: the Samaritan eschatological figure, otherwise called the Taheb, and usually identified with the returning Moses. He is not specifically called
by this name here, nor is he overtly identified with Moses, although it is suggested that he will have Moses' staff with him.

---

26. Gaster was of the opinion that the concluding verses prophesied a second turning away. Asatir, p. 310. The text is not
clear, and Ben-Hayyim suggests otherwise. spr ’styr, 15, 84.
Gaster was following the outlines of Samaritan eschatology suggested by the 14th century Shira Yetima.

27. spr ’styr, 15, 86.

28. Adler and Seligsohn, "Nouvelle Chronique samaritaine,"
191-201; Gaster, "Chain of Samaritan High Priests," 493-494.
S. J. Miller, The Samaritan Molad Mosheh, (New York: Philosophical Library, 1949), p. 246.

28a. cf. the medieval Slavonic Ladder of Jacob, which represents the future history of the lawless age as a period of twenty-four kings. M. R. James, Lost Apocrypha of the Old Testament
(London: SPCK, 1920), p. 98.

29. See Ben-Hayyim, spr ’styr, 15, 85.

It should be noted that the three princes preceding the final prince are also described as persons who will accomplish good things for Israel. It is possible that these were four allusions to one person, by way of poetic parallelism, rather than four distinct princes. There are other examples in the text where the same observation could apply. If this was the case, then the original poem was not meant to suggest a prophecy of twenty-four (or twenty-six) successive rulers, but a much shorter number which was either misunderstood or distorted by the writer who added the concluding verse. It may be that the editor who wrote the final verse was the writer also of the prose account in Chapter XI, and that he used this (older?) poem to add a literary dimension to his otherwise drab writing.

In its present form, the Asaṭir regards Moses as representing a position in the center of time: twenty-six righteous men before him; twenty-six princes (some good and some bad) after him; 2796 years prior to his death, 3204 years thereafter. His life represents the high point of human history: all which precedes it leads up to it; that which follows is a tragic descent. There is no element of wonder associated with Moses' death itself, the element of wonder is to be found in the prophecy delivered before his death. The prophet viewed the vistas of future history and declared the things which would come to pass.

GASTER'S "DEATH OF MOSES"

When Moses Gaster published his edition of the Asaṭir, he included also a text which he entitled a "Samaritan Story of the Death of Moses".[30] Gaster found this text in a Samaritan chronicle, one of a number of manuscripts bearing the title Sefer Hayyamim.[31] He regarded it as being drawn from an ancient account, and incorporated it into the chronicle for the sake of completeness. Although he noted its similarities to Marqah, he did not believe Marqah to be its ultimate source. He suggested that it represented part of an ancient comprehensive story of Moses' death, of which materials in the Asaṭir were also a part.[32] There was a certain logic to Gaster's claim, suggested as it no doubt was by the model of Jewish pseudepigraphical writings. Gaster's "Samaritan Story of the Death of Moses" would be a writing which could be compared to the Jewish Assumption of Moses (lost, but known in part from Patristic sources), as the last chapters of the Asaṭir might be compared to the Jewish Testament of Moses.

In spite of Gaster's attempt to establish antiquity for this text by reference to parallels in Josephus and Pseudo-Philo, even a casual reading of it reveals that it is basically an abridgment of Memar Marqah V. 2-3, to which the author has added some additional materials by way of introduction. The text is, however, not without significance, although for reasons which did

---

30. Asatir, pp. 55-59 of the Aramaic-Hebrew section; translation on pp. 303-321.

31. Gaster's Codex 1168 (=John Rylands' Codex 259). See Edward Robertson, Catalogue of Samaritan Manuscripts in the John Rylands Library, Manchester, vol. II, The Gaster Manuscripts (Manchester: John Rylands Library, 1962), cols. 185-186.

32. Asatir, pp. 178-182.

not occur to Gaster. Although the writer followed the outline of Marqah, employing the actual clichés of his source, he selectively edited the materials. It is in his treatment of Joshua that this writer has deviated most conspicuously from his source. An example of this is the omission of the passage in Marqah which states that the Fānûtâ will come because of Joshua! Such a statement would be inconsistent with what this later editor wished to stress. References in Marqah to Joshua without titular ascription become in this text references to "our master" or "the master" Joshua (h'dwn yhwš'). When Joshua goes to inform Eleazar, Ithamar, and Phinehas of the imminent death of Moses, the priests address him as the "Leader of the Elect of the Hebrews." (mšrt dm' bny 'br),[33] a detail lacking in Marqah. In the final farewell of Moses at his ascent on Nebo, Marqah notes that the three priests and Joshua kissed the face of Moses, whereas all others kissed his hand. In this text, only Joshua is accorded the honor of kissing Moses' face. In the parting hymn of peace upon Moses offered by Joshua, the statement contained in Marqah that there would not again arise one like Moses is conspicuous by its absence. Finally, at the conclusion of his account, the editor has added an encomium on Joshua rather than Moses!

In addition to those alterations by which Joshua was magnified, there is another significant deviation from Marqah by this editor. It is said that at the moment of Moses' death his "holy spirit departed in his breath." (wys't rwhw hqdš b'nšmh), and the angels were commanded to take up his spirit. Marqah states simply that Moses' nefeš departed, and has no account of any experience of his soul or spirit after death. This may reflect a more complex view of man's spiritual nature than that held by Marqah, or a more exalted view of Moses' glorification.

Although this tradition can be no older than the 4th century C.E., there may be some truth to Gaster's claim that it is older than the modern text in which he found it. As for its provenience, it quite obviously derives from that circle within Samaritanism which stressed the significance of Joshua, against the position represented by Marqah. This would appear to have been the same circle from which the Samaritan Arabic Book of Joshua derived.

THE SAMARITAN ARABIC BOOK OF JOSHUA

The first Samaritan chronicle to come to the attention of Western scholars was an Arabic text treating the period from the investiture of Joshua to the time of Baba Rabba. Inasmuch as two-thirds of this text is concerned with Joshua, the work has appropriately been called the Samaritan Book of Joshua.[34] Other Samaritan chronicles containing Joshua materials (in both Hebrew and Arabic) subsequently came to light, some of which gave evi-

---

33. Gaster translates, "Minister of the Excellence of the children of Eber." Ibid, p. 305. My translation follows Cowley's suggestion for dm', in his glossary to the Samaritan liturgy, The Samaritan Liturgy, p. liv. The term m^{e}šārēt is used for Joshua in Biblical Hebrew. I have interpreted "minister" as a title of leadership.

34. Scaligers' 16th century text, published by Juynboll. See note 6.

dence of being dependent upon this Arabic recension,[35] and others which appeared to be related to other recensional traditions.[36] It is difficult to escape the conclusion that the Samaritan community possessed at some early date an autonomous Book of Joshua which was in time utilized by copyists for the first part of longer chronological accounts. It is not easy, however, to determine which of the various collections of Joshua materials in the several chronicles might be representative of the earliest stage in textual history of such an independent writing, nor is it easy to determine the relationships of the various extant recensions to one another (if they are indeed related at all).[37] Only one of the Samaritan chronicles containing Joshua materials (of those which have been published) includes a detailed account of the death of Moses. This is the original Arabic chronicle discovered in the 16th century by Joseph Scaliger and published by T. G. J. Juynboll in 1848.[38] Juynboll was confident that this text was a copy of a work written in the mid-13th century. The author of the chronicle states that his work was a translation into Arabic from older Hebrew texts, and there is no reason to doubt this. To avoid confusing this work with portions of other Samaritan chronicles, it shall be referred to as the Arabic Book of Joshua, not withstanding its alleged Hebrew sources.

The Arabic Book of Joshua begins with the account of the investiture of Joshua with the caliphate by Moses. Joshua is the hero of the work, and this fact is established at the very beginning: Joshua is commissioned to be Moses' successor and to lead the people in the conquest of Canaan; Moses imparts to Joshua knowledge of hidden things to enable him to fulfill his role of leadership; and a covenant is made whereby this position is firmly established. All of this is performed in the presence of Eleazar the priest, and thus appears to be an expansion of the biblical account of Numbers 27:18-23. This is followed, anachronistically, with an account of the Balaam affair, then of Israel's dealings with Midian, and finally with an account of Moses' death and Joshua's speech following that death. Joshua's role at the death of Moses is clearly understood in the light of his previous investiture of authority and leadership by Moses.

---

35. So Abu'l Fath. see note 6.

36. So Moses Gaster, "Das Buch Josua in hebräisch-samaritanischer Rezension," ZDMG, 62 (1908), 209-279, 494-549. A text in this recension was also published by D. Yellin in Jerusalem in 1902. The texts of Gaster and Yellin are used in the Joshua part of Macdonald's Samaritan Chronicle No. II (see pp. 70-74).

37. A recent attempt to resolve these thorny problems is found in A. D. Crown, "New Light on the Inter-Relationships of Samaritan Chronicles from some Manuscripts in the John Rylands' Library."

38. Crown reports that Rylands MS 374 (Gaster MS 1167) contains two distinct accounts of Moses' death, one which agrees with the Scaliger account and one which does not. Unfortunately, Crown gives no details of this alternate tradition, and I have not had access to this manuscript. "Some Traces of Heterodox Theology in the Samaritan Book of Joshua,", BJRL, 50 (1967), 183. I have reason to think, from what Crown relates about the context of this account, that this other story is that which I report below, in the section entitled "A Death of Moses from the Barton Collection."

This account of Moses' death agrees for the most part, up to a particular point, with the account preserved in Marqah, although it is much shorter. Moses gives instructions to Joshua, the priests, and the elders; trumpets are sounded and heralds go forth to announce his death; Moses instructs the people from an exalted seat, telling them of the days of the Rāhūtâ and the Fānūtâ, of the deluge of fire and the Day of Vengeance and Reward, and of what would happen in the course of Israelite history (with no specific details given). Moses then ascends Mt. Nebo with Joshua, Eleazar, and the elders, but with much less pomp and ceremony than in Marqah's account. It is at this point that the account deviates from the story of Moses' death in Marqah. According to this tradition, night began to fall and the pillar of fire separated Moses from the view of the people, after which no one knew what happened to him. It is stated that after that time Moses' dealings were directly with the Lord and his angels; it is not specifically stated that he died![39] In the song of Joshua which follows, it is noted that Moses' departure was unique; from the time of Adam, everyone's death had been witnessed and the grave known, but no one knows Moses' grave. One is reminded of the statement in the Testament of Moses that all men have sepulchres on earth, but for Moses the world is his sepulchre (11:809). One is reminded also, although the situation is not entirely analogous, of the New Testament tradition of the empty tomb of Jesus (especially that in Mark's Gospel).

The speech of Joshua which follows the account of Moses' departure (death?) is rich in encomia on the Prophet. It contains a set of ten rhetorical questions on the incomparable greatness of Moses ("What other prophet...," "Who else..." etc., etc.), followed by ten vocative epithets expressing his magnificence. The language is similar to that of Marqah, and similar also to the encomia contained in the later Samaritan traditions celebrating the birth of Moses.[40] Although the epithets extol Moses for

---

39. Ginzberg makes a point of noting that in the Jewish traditions the death of Moses takes place in daylight, in public view, and suggests that this was "to combat the view that he did not die at all, but was translated to heaven." Legends of the Jews vol. VI, 151-152. If the Samaritan Arabic Book of Joshua did not intend to suggest the latter, it is possible that it drew from a literary source which did! Ginzberg cites several Jewish sources which note the opinion held by some that "Moses did not die, but continues to minister above." Legends of the Jews, VI, 161-162. The idea of Moses reigning in heaven, as a kind of King of Paradise, ministering unto God and for man, is found in late Samaritan writings. See, for example, the story of Ibrāhīm al-Qabāṣī's vision, in Gaster, Samaritan Eschatology, pp. 200-201, and the vision of Ṣadaqah the Physician, in Robertson, Catalogue of Samaritan Manuscripts, II, col. 168. See also Macdonald, Theology of the Samaritans, p. 414; Montgomery, The Samaritans, p. 227. cf. also Josephus, Antiquities IV. 326, where it is stated that Moses himself wrote of his death out of fear that it might be said "that by reason of his surpassing virtue he had gone back to the deity." (Thackery's translation, Loeb edn.) Pseudo-Philo also states quite clearly that Moses died. (Antiquities XIX. 16.)

40. See, for example, the long set of such rhetorical questions in the Aramaic Molad Mosheh: S. J. Miller, The Samaritan Molad Mosheh. (New York: Philosophical Library, 1949), pp. 308-322. cf. also the parallel material in the 16th century Arabic Maulid an-Nashi of Ismā'īl ar-Rumaihī: Ibid, pp. 168-182.

various feats in the span of his long career, the rhetorical questions by which his uniqueness is stressed center on what Moses had experienced previously on Mt. Sinai. In this account, as in Marqah's, the ascent on Mt. Nebo is seen as paralleling that on Mt. Sinai.[41] It may not be said that the final ascent is represented as being greater in significance than the former. Indeed, just the opposite appears to be the case. It is because Moses had ascended into the heavenly realms at Sinai, that his final ascent on Mt. Nebo was invested with meaning: "Where is one, who has trodden the fire, and cleft the darkness, and rent the clouds, and reached into the curtain of omnipotence, beside thee?"

A DEATH OF MOSES FROM THE BARTON COLLECTION

There is a brief account of the death of Moses preserved in a manuscript in the W. E. Barton collection in the Mugar Library of Boston University. The manuscript was secured from the modern Samaritan community during the period in which Moses Gaster was also building his collection.[42] It consists of thirty-one pages in Arabic and fifty-eight pages in Samaritan Hebrew. The work was falsely identified by Barton as being an edition of the Book of Joshua discovered by Scaliger. The Hebrew section is entitled Sefer Hayyamim; it belongs to the recension of materials concerning Joshua previously published by Gaster and Macdonald. The Arabic material is untitled. The first nine and one-half pages of this section contain an Arabic version of a story concerning the spies which Gaster had discovered in a Hebrew text.[43] Pages ten through twelve contain an account of Moses' death which the writer claims to be a condensation of Marqah. This appears to be the case. The work may thus be compared to Gaster's "Death of Moses", from his codex 1168. Unlike Gaster's text, however, this account does not reflect an attempt to edit in reference to the Scaliger-Juynboll recension of the Book of Joshua. Just the opposite is the case.

In this account, Joshua plays no role at all. Only Eleazar is mentioned specifically by name. The account follows a ceremony which takes place before the wagon or mobile bier containing the body of Joseph, and Moses' final address is directed as much to Joseph as to the assembled congregation. This is consistent with the Moses-Joseph linkage which is found elsewhere in Marqah. The account of the experience on the summit of Nebo contains a curious tradition not noted in the other sources reviewed here: Moses removes his veil in the presence of the Pillar of Cloud, and all of the people marvel at the brightness of his countenance, brighter even than the sun. It is specifically sta-

---

41. See also the late Samaritan Yom al-Din, where the giving of the oration of Deut. 32 is compared to Moses' experience at Sinai. Gaster, Samaritan Eschatology, p. 125.

42. On the Barton collection and its history, see my "Studies on the Samaritan Materials in the W. E. Barton Collection in the Boston University Library," Proceedings of the Fifth World Congress of Jewish Studies, vol. I (Jerusalem: World Union of Jewish Studies, 1972), pp. 134-143.

43. Moses Gaster, "The Samaritan Hebrew Sources of the Arabic Book of Joshua," Journal of the Royal Asiatic Society (1930), 567-599.

ted that when the Cloud separated Moses from the view of the
people, all knew that he had died. Nothing more is said of
what happened to Moses after this point.

THE DEATH OF MOSES AND THE BIRTH OF MOSES

In the Samaritan sources reviewed thus far, it is clear that
Moses' death was not viewed in isolation, but within the context
of the totality of that which his life represented. His death
was the culminating experience of his life-work, of which the
receiving of the Torah on Horeb was the focal point. For at
least one writer (the author of the Asatir), Moses' life represented the central point of human history. For two other writers, the life-work of Moses was strongly linked to the career of
Joshua (Gaster's "Death of Moses" and the Arabic Book of Joshua).
It was not so much Moses' death which was celebrated in the accounts of his experience on Mt. Nebo as it was his life. It
should come as no surprise, then, that just as Moses' death was
a subject of interest to Samaritan liturgists and theologians,
so too was his birth - the two being the termina of that life.
In the Samaritan literary and theological renascence of the 14th
century and following, traditions glorifying the Prophet came to
center upon events associated with his birth and infancy. A Samaritan festival on the birthday of the Prophet on the 15th of
Nisan became popular, and the liturgical materials created for
it came to be used on other joyous occasions as well. The popu-
larity of the Samaritan celebration of Moses' birth has been attributed to both Moslem and Christian influence, but the real
reason probably lies in the basic human experience of joy experienced at the birth of a child. Also, one of the important developing theological concepts of Samaritanism was the doctrine
of Moses as the Light of the World. It was on the occasion of
his birth that the community could joyously celebrate the embod-
iment in Moses of the Light which had come into the world in Adam and had been transmitted through a chain of righteous men to
his time.

Although aggadic traditions and liturgical ascriptions concerning Moses' birth and infancy are found in the early writings
of Marqah, and also in the Asatir, the greatest amount of such
material is contained in the Molad Mosheh corpus of texts, from
the 14th century to the 19th century.[44] In these writings, the
death of Moses is not ignored, but - with one notable exception -
touched upon only briefly in liturgical ascriptions.[45] The one

---

44. These include the followings: (1) a poem by Jacob the
rabban of Damascus (14th century): T. H. Gaster, "A Samaritan
Poem about Moses," in A. Berger, et.al., The Joshua Bloch Memorial vol. : Studies in Booklore and History (New York: New York
Public Library, 1960), pp. 115-139. (2) An acrostic hymn by Ab-
dallah ben Salāmah (14th century): Cowley, Samaritan Liturgy,
746-753. (3) The Arabic treatise Maulid an-Nashī by Ismaʿīl
ar-Rumaihī of Damascus (16th century): Selig J. Miller, The
Samaritan Molad Mosheh, pp. 56-203. (4) The Samaritan Aramaic
Molad Mosheh of Phinehas ben Isaac (late 19th century): Ibid,
pp. 232-353. (5) There are some Molad Mosheh poems attributed
to Ghazāl al-Duwaik (12th-13th century): See Gaster, Samaritan
Eschatology, p. 71; Macdonald, Theology of the Samaritans, pp.
45-46.

45. See, for example, Miller, Molad Mosheh, pp. 168-182. It
is interesting to note that the elements which are said by Mar-

Molad Mosheh text which devotes considerable attention to Moses' death is the 14th century Hebrew poem by Jacob the rabban of Damascus. In the literary structure of the work, the life of the Prophet is briefly encompassed from birth to death, with the receiving of the law on Sinai being the median point, and with Moses being glorified on all three occasions.

The following are the basic elements in Jacob's account of Moses' death: When the Israelites reached the plain of Moab, Moses knew that the day of his departure had come. His sole request was that he should see the Mount of Inheritance, Gerizim. Instead, God showed him the whole extent of the land which had been made for his sake (an allusion to Deut. 34:1-2 in the Samaritan reading, which refers to a greater area than does MT - from the Nile to the Euphrates).[46] On the day God declared he should die, Moses gathered the people for blessing. They besought him that he remain and lead them into the land of their fathers, but he replied that he had no inheritance in that land. (In this, there is no reference to Joshua.) In his ascent, the angels walked before him and behind him and a cloud enveloped him. The angels wept and offered a song of praise to Moses as the Prophet of God and as Priest for the angels.[47] The song of the angels consists of ten ascriptions to Moses, each beginning with ʾth, "Thou art...", celebrating the uniqueness of the Prophet as the recipient of the Divine Light. The poem ends with the clear statement that Moses died (ʾth mt ʾh mšh) and that he was buried in the valley of Beth Peor. His tomb will remain unknown until the Day of Judgment, and a prayer is offered that he be restored on that Day to serve as intercessor, and as Priest in the Divine Worship.

The death of Moses in Jacob's poem is not a joyous occasion. The angels weep at this time, in contrast to their rejoicing after his birth. Jacob's account differs in this respect from both Marqah and the Arabic Book of Joshua, where the angels rejoice at Moses' appearance. It stands in marked contrast to the Arabic Book of Joshua on the nature of Moses' departure. In Jacob's poem, Moses does not go to be with the angels, but he dies and is buried in hope of his resurrection on the Day of Judgment. The difference in the two accounts may reflect different understandings within the Samaritan community of the doctrine of the future life.

COMMON AND DISPARATE ELEMENTS IN THE TRADITIONS

One cannot review the major Samaritan traditions on Moses' death without being impressed by two facts: the first is that there appears to be a common pattern or basic framework to all

qah to have glorified Moses at his death are said by the Aramaic Molad Mosheh of Phinehas ben Isaac to have glorified him at his birth.

46. Did Pseudo-Philo also know this reading? See Antiquities XIX. 10.

47. Compare Pseudo-Philo, Antiquities XIX. 16, where the day of Moses' death is represented as the saddest day of history. The angels not only wept on that occasion (as in Jacob's account), but ceased in the offering of their daily hymn (contra Jacob).

of the stories; the second is that within this framework there are significant differences. How is one to explain both the common and the disparate elements?

The following may be regarded as the essential outline of the story of Moses' death in the Samaritan texts:

1. Moses receives word of his impending death, and accepts this without complaint, although great remorse is expressed by others (be they creatures of nature, angels, or Israelites). If Moses expresses regret, it is for the sake of Israel.

2. Moses offers worship to God, and announces his departure to an inner-circle of associates, including Joshua and the priests.

3. The people are assembled for blessing, instruction, and farewells, in the course of which Moses indicates what will occur in the future.

4. Final words and tearful farewells are given, after which Moses ascends Mt. Nebo.

5. Moses is accompanied in his ascent, either by his close associates or by angels, and is visible to the mourning people assembled below.

6. Hymns of praise are offered to Moses (either by the people, Joshua, or angels.)

7. Moses is glorified on the summit of Nebo by representatives of the heavenly order, who obstruct (either by Cloud or Fire), his view by the people, after which his activities are unknown to them. It is affirmed that Moses viewed the land, and that the exact location of his tomb is unknown.

8. Further words of praise are offered to Moses.

All of the texts surveyed here agree essentially with this pattern, or, if they do not contain all of its elements, do not contradict it. The earliest witness to this literary framework in the Samaritan texts is Marqah. It is quite obvious, however, that he did not create it. The outline is essentially that which is found in Josephus, <u>Antiquities</u> IV. 315-331, although the Jewish historian lacks element 6, and the glorification of Moses is not developed in number 7. This is not to infer that Marqah was directly dependent upon Josephus, or, conversely, that Josephus had been dependent upon an older Samaritan writing. Although either possibility may be entertained, it is just as likely that Josephus and Marqah were both dependent upon a common old Palestinian story of the death of Moses. Each told the story in his own way, with Marqah and the other Samaritan writers glorifying Moses to a greater degree than did Josephus.

Later Samaritan writers who followed this pattern probably did so because of literary dependence upon Marqah, although it is not out of the question that the outline of the story existed within the community independently of Marqah's writings. In either case, the common elements in the death of Moses accounts are easily explained. The disparate elements, however, represent a distinct problem. It might be argued that this is no problem at all, and should perhaps be expected in a collection of texts of a variety of literary type, in prose and poetry, in three languages, written over a span of a millennium. Although these are important considerations which could well explain incidental variations in details, there are none the less many dissimilarities which reflect significant differences of opinion on theological issues. It is difficult to avoid the conclusion that a number of the disparate elements in the stories were intentional variations for the sake of promoting particular theological positions. Among these theological issues were (1) the question of the succession to Moses, and (2) the doctrine of the future life.

Although Joshua plays an important role in Marqah's account of the death of Moses, there is definitely a conscious attempt to downgrade his significance. Joshua is in the company of the three priests, Eleazar, Ithamar, and Phinehas when the people are summoned to learn of Moses' departure, and with the same three in the ascent on Mt. Nebo (with Eleazar and Phinehas accorded the honor of taking Moses' hands). In Moses' final words, Joshua is informed that the Apostasy will come because of him, and Moses expresses the conviction that things would be better if only he or Aaron or Eleazar could be present in the future. After this statement, Marqah includes a hymn of praise to Moses, likening the great Prophet to Jacob (again Joshua loses by comparison). Elsewhere in Marqah there is a linkage between Joseph and Moses.[48] The poem of Jacob the rabban does not mention Joshua at all, nor does he figure in Moses' final testament in the Asaṭir (Asaṭir XI. 1-2 being unrelated to the testament itself). The same may be said for Joshua in the account of Moses' death in the Barton manuscript, where, again, we find the Moses-Joseph linkage rather than Moses-Joshua. In contrast, the Arabic Book of Joshua and Gaster's "Death of Moses", promote Joshua as the chosen successor of Moses, and maintain his preeminence among his peers and his positive relationship to his predecessor. This contrast is particularly evident in Gaster's "Death of Moses", where the writer has edited Marqah's account to bring it into agreement with the theological position represented in the Book of Joshua.

It may be more than coincidental that the same writings which agree with one another on Joshua's importance, agree also on Moses' state after death. Both the Arabic Book of Joshua and Gaster's "Death of Moses" represent Moses' death as being the end of his time among men and the beginning of his time with the angels. For these writers, death is an ascent of the spirit into the heavenly realm. The Book of Joshua ends with the prayer that God "would unite us to him through his mercy." For Marqah and Jacob, Moses' death is a burial in a hidden sepulchre in hope of the Day of Judgment.[49] In Marqah it is knowledge of what will happen after that Day that sustains Moses and removes from him the fear of death. Jacob's poem ends with the petition that God would raise up Moses on that Day, that he may establish true worship and intercede for his people. It is evident that two different views of life after death are expressed here.

Although Samaritanism in modern times has been a unitive religious system, it is evident from a number of sources that the Samaritan community contained within it, over a long period of time, a variety of theological schools in competition with one

---

48. See note 7. cf., also, A. D. Crown, "Some Traces of Heterodox Theology in the Samaritan Book of Joshua," 185-186.

49. The statement in Memar Marqah V. 3 that Moses ascended "from human status to that of the angels" does not refer to his condition after death, but to his experience in his earlier ascent and glorification on Sinai.

another. The Samaritan chronicles and Christian writings bear witness to the existence of a number of Samaritan sects, of which the largest and most influential was the Dosithean. This sect was long-lived (there may have been several Dosithean sects at different times), and was at one time in its history associated with the sect of Simon Magus. In recent times, John Bowman has argued that Dositheanism represented a lay movement in Samaritanism which began to gain ascendancy over the orthodox Samaritan priesthood in the time of Baba Rabba and that the synagogue was the institutional base of this heterodox movement. Both the priestly orthodox and the lay Dositheans remained in tension with one another until the 14th century, when an accomodation was made between them, and a new Samaritan orthodoxy (with a new liturgy) came into being.[50] H. G. Kippenberg has followed a number of Bowman's suggestions concerning the Dositheans and the synagogue in his traditionsgeschichtliche study of Samaritan traditions in the Aramaic literature.[51] Bowman has also been followed by his student A. D. Crown, who has reviewed a number of Samaritan writings to discern traces of heterodox (cautiously identified as Dosithean) theology.[52] His study has led him to conclude that the Arabic (perhaps originally Hebrew-Aramaic) Book of Joshua originated in lay, heterodox circles with a strong theology of Joshua, and that Marqah's writings reflect the anti-Joshua theology of the priestly dominated orthodoxy.[53] Crown also contends that the Asatir represents a priestly counter-blast to the heterodox theology. Crown and Bowman differ in their assessment of Marqah's place in the priestly-lay conflict: Bowman regards Marqah as a Dosithean; Crown sees him as fitting into the orthodox priestly circles.[54]

The hypothesis of lay-priestly conflict in the Samaritan community provides a situation against which the disparate elements in the death of Moses traditions may be understood, particularly in regard to the issue of Moses' succession. Whether the lay

---

50. John Bowman, "The Importance of Samaritan Researches," pp. 43-54; "Pilgrimage to Mount Gerizim," pp. 17-28. This brief summary does not do full justice to the complexity of the historical dialectic Bowman develops.

51. Garizim und Synagoge, pp. 175-349.

52. Crown, "Some Traces of Heterodox Theology in the Samaritan Book of Joshua;" "New Light on the Inter-Relationships of Samaritan Chronicles," esp. 308-311; "Dositheans, Resurrection and a Messianic Joshua," Antichthon, 1 (1967-1968). I regret that I have not had access to this last work.

53. To be more specific, Joshua was associated with the Taheb in Dosithean circles, with the orthodox, priestly theology, associating Joseph with the Samaritan eschatological figure. "Heterodox Theology in the Samaritan Book of Joshua," 185-186, 195-197. In support of this, see the Joseph-Taheb connection in Memar Marqah IV, 12. Crown makes the interesting observation that the Joshua-Jesus typology in Justin Martyr was an application to Christian theology of Samaritan Dosithean views." "New Light on the Inter-Relationships of Samaritan Chronicles," p. 309.

54. Bowman, "Importance of Samaritan Researches," p. 50; Crown, "Heterodox Theology in the Samaritan Book of Joshua," p. 186.

circles in which the pro-Joshua traditions were maintained may be designated Dosithean is another matter. It has been noted that texts which agree in regard to Moses' succession agree also on the nature of the future life. Inasmuch as it is known that the doctrine of the future life was an issue of contention between the orthodox and the Dositheans, it may well be that this designation is correct.[55] It is the opinion of this writer, however, that a clearer picture of the Dositheans must first emerge before such identifications may be made with any degree of certainty.[56]

THE SAMARITAN TRADITIONS AND THE PSEUDEPIGRAPHICAL LITERATURE: THE ASSUMPTION OF MOSES AND THE TESTAMENT OF MOSES

Light may be thrown upon Samaritan accounts of Moses' death in the pro-Joshua texts (Book of Joshua and Gaster Codex 1168) by materials preserved in some early Christian writings usually identified as fragments of the lost Assumption of Moses. Both Clement of Alexandria and Origen cite a tradition (identified by Origen as being from a non-canonical work, not specified by title) that two Moseses were seen at his death, the one a living spiritual Moses who was transported to heaven by the angels, the other a dead corporeal Moses who was buried. A variant of this tradition is cited by Evodius, Bishop of Uzala, in a letter to Augustine. Evodius claims the story was found in the "apocryphal and secret books of Moses himself, which is writing without authority" (apocryphis et in secretis ipsius Moysi, quae scriptura caret auctoritate...).[57] This tradition corresponds closely to the Samaritan account in Gaster's "Death of Moses", where Moses' body was interred in a cave, while his "holy spirit" was taken up by angels. The story was cited by Clement and Origen as providing an analogy for the interpretation of scripture, the literal text corresponding to the dead body of Moses, the spiritual meaning comparable to the "Moses who lives in the spirit" (Origen). Clement states also that Joshua perceived the spiritual Moses, whereas his colleague Caleb did not, Joshua being a spiritual man. Although the detail concerning Caleb is lacking in our Samaritan texts, the glorification of Joshua as a spiritual man is a conspicuous feature.

---

55. According to Bowman, the view of Moses' death in the post-14th century liturgy (the new Defter, which represented an accommodation between Dositheans and orthodox views) was that "he did not die but ascended on high." "Pilgrimage to Mt. Gerizim", p.22. Bowman suggests this was due to the influence of the Memar Marqah. I would suggest rather that this reflects the theology represented in the Book of Joshua. According to Ab'ul Fath, one of the heresies established by Dusis and his follower Levi was that as soon as a man is buried he rises and goes to Paradise. Vilmar, Abulfathi Annales Samaritani, p. 157.

56. This remark is offered with all deference and respect for the work of Crown and Bowman, and with acknowledgment of indebtedness, but with a cautious reserve in regard to the conjectural nature of many of their conclusions. Recent conversations with Mr. Stanley Isser of New York suggest that his research on the early history of the Dositheans will make a major contribution in this regard.

57. Clement of Alexandria, Stromata VI. 15; Origen, Homily on Joshua II. 2; Evodius, Epistle 258. See A. M. Denis, Intro-

This is the only instance in which Samaritan traditions on Moses' death agree with texts generally recognized as Assumption of Moses fragments. There is no correspondence in the Samaritan stories with the more characteristic features of the Assumption: no role of the Archangel Michael, no claim for the body of Moses by Satan, no contest between Michael and Satan, etc.[58] It may be, however, that the writing cited by Clement, Origen, and Evodius was not the Assumption of Moses, i.e. the writing which contained the Michael-Satan story. Neither Clement nor Origen identified his source, and Evodius does not cite a work of that title. The identification of these fragments with the Análēpsis Mōseōs appears to be based on the subject with which they are concerned (the ascent of the spiritual Moses), and perhaps also on the use of the verb analambánō by Clement. If these Christian writers were dependent on the Assumption of Moses, this particular section of that work may represent a tradition preserved in Jewish circles paralleling a tradition preserved also in certain Samaritan circles. If the source was not the Assumption of Moses, it could well have been an early Jewish or Samaritan writing of the sort we have seen in medieval Samaritan texts: a text magnifying both Moses and Joshua, and reflecting a particular understanding of spiritual life beyond death.

Samaritan stories on the death of Moses invite comparison also to the pseudepigraphical Testament of Moses. This is true not only of the pro-Joshua texts, but of Marqah and the Asaṭir as well. Of these, the Asaṭir is closest in literary type. The pro-Joshua texts represent a theology of Moses and Joshua which is essentially that found in the Testament, while all of our texts are in agreement with this pseudepigraphon on its theology of Moses.

The following affirmations concerning Moses in the Testament are in agreement with what was understood or said about him in the Samaritan writings: He is the one prepared from the foundation of the earth to be the mediator of God's covenant (TM 1:14); the one to whom the hidden knowledge of the secret of the future is given, and through whom it is revealed (2:3-10:15); the one who does not weep for himself at his death, but for others (11:2-4); the Sacred Spirit worthy of the Lord, manifold and incomprehensible, the Lord of the Word, faithful in all, God's Chief Prophet, the Perfect Teacher, etc. Similarly, the following affirmations in the Testament of Moses concerning Joshua are consistent with what was understood of him in the pro-Joshua texts: Joshua is the successor of Moses as leader of the people and as guardian of the sacred things (1:7 and 10:15),[59] the one who was

---

duction aux Pseudépigraphes Grecs d' Ancien Testament (Leiden: E. J. Brill, 1970), pp. 131-132; M. R. James, Lost Apocrypha of the Old Testament (London: SPCK, 1920), pp. 44-45; R. H. Charles, The Assumption of Moses (London: Adam and Charles Black, 1897), pp. 107-108. This tradition contrasts with the point of view expressed by Philo of Alexandria, that Moses' body and soul were united into a single entity of pure spirit or mind which ascended to heaven. De Vita Mosis II. 288.

58. A story such as this would be atypical of Samaritan folklore. Satan does not figure in Samaritan theology as the archenemy of God as the Evil Power.

59. The term successor plebi in T.M. 1:7 is most likely from the Hebrew mešārēt hāʿām, and connotes servant or minister as a title of leadership. So Charles, Assumption of Moses, 56; Apocrypha and Pseudepigrapha (Oxford: Clarendon Press, 1913, vol.

commissioned to bring the people into the land, because he was a
man of courage and blameless before God (1:10); the one entrusted with the keeping and preservation of the sacred writings (1:
17-18); he who would bless the people in the land, give them
their share in the inheritance, establish the kingdom, and ap-
point magistrates (2:1-2): the one to whom the mystery of the
future was entrusted (2:3-10:15); and the one who received per-
sonally from Moses the assurance that he could accomplish the
overwhelming task of leading and caring for the people which Moses had led (compare 11:1-19 with 1:1-13). This understanding
is not only consistent with the pro-Joshua stories of Moses'
death, but also with the accounts of Joshua's leadership throughout the Book of Joshua (in its several recensions). Of particular interest is the statement in T.M. 1:17-18 that Joshua should
carefully preserve the sacred writings and deposit them in the
place which God had chosen from the beginning of creation for
his worship (which would continue to serve that function until
the consummation of time). Although I can find no specific Samaritan text containing such a command, the language is quite
typical of Samaritan statements concerning Mt. Gerizim. Indeed,
if the statement in the Testament of Moses is to be correlated
with the biblical account, the logical place for such deposit
would have been Shechem (so Joshua 24 - unless the tradition in
Judges 1:8-9 is followed to make a claim for Jerusalem). The
Deuteronomic tradition, in chapters 27-28, also strongly suggests
Shechem/Gerizim (esp. in the Samaritan reading of Deut. 27:4).
Also of interest is the statement in the Testament that Joshua
will establish a kingdom (eis regnum). This corresponds to the
Samaritan designation of Joshua as King (in the Book of Joshua,
but compare the Joseph the King traditions in Marqah).

In addition to these similarities in the understanding of the
theological significance of Moses and Joshua, there are also several aspects of the prognostication of Moses in the Testament
which may be compared to elements in the Samaritan stories. The
prophecy of future events by Moses in the Samaritan texts is concerned with either one of two things, or both: (1) the apostasy
which will bring about the Fānûtâ, the age of Divine Disfavor,
and (2) the final consummation of things before the Day of Judgment. Of the various Samaritan texts, only the Asaṭir attempts
to trace future history with any attention to detail, with the
remarks of the prose account being fairly straightforward, and the
poetic account being highly cryptic. The following are points
at which there are similarities between the Testament of Moses
and the Asaṭir: the troubles of Israel will begin several years
after the people enter the land of Canaan, when two tribes shall
transfer the testimony of the tabernacle (T.M. 2:4a, following
the unemended Latin text). So too Asaṭir XI. 21-25, where a new
sanctuary will be established to which Judah and Benjamin will
give allegiance. The difference between the points of view in
the Testament and the Asaṭir is that for the former the sanctuary
of the two tribes is the legitimate shrine, and for the latter
it is an apostate sanctuary. In the Testament of Moses, the history of the two groups (the two tribes and the ten tribes) is
then traced, with special attention given to the sin of the ten
tribes which brings about the devastation of the land, including
the destruction of the sacred temple, and exile. This compares
to Asaṭir XI. 26-33, where the Samaritan writer recites the sin

---

II, p. 414. On the use of this as a title for Joshua in a Samaritan text, see note 33. The expression mihi successorum in
10:15, however, would appear to mean "my successor" (with Charles
in his 1897 translation; against Charles in his 1913 publication).

of the apostate people, in this case the two tribes, to the time of the destruction of the apostate shrine. Both the Testament of Moses and the Asatir treat subsequent history as a period during which troubles will be multiplied through a succession of kings (compare T.M. 5:1; 6:1-2; 8:1 with Asatir XII). In the Testament, the time of trouble will end with the appearance of a priestly martyr; in the Asatir it will end with the appearance of a righteous prince. In each document, the last ruler before the coming of the new age will be a despot who will prohibit circumcision. (T.M. 8:1-3; Asatir XII. 20).

Although the two writings appear to follow a common pattern, there is a basic difference between them in their understanding of what part of the Israelite nation constitutes the people of God. It is this understanding which distinguishes the Testament of Moses as a Jewish writing. There is, however, at least one scholar who has suggested that the Testament of Moses was a Samaritan product.[60] K. H. Haacker has argued that the origin of the Testament of Moses was in the Mosaic religion of the Samaritans, who regarded themselves as the true Israel and not a sect, and who were representative of the Deuteronomic tradition in which the Testament stands: The central cultus in this writing, following the old Deuteronomic theology, is Shechem (T.M. 1:17). Although there are references to Jerusalem and its temple in the document, these do not indicate that its author was a Jew, nor are they representative of a Zion-theology. In fact it is not the Jerusalem shrine (as one might at first think) that is referred to as the sanctuary of the two tribes, but the Gerizim sanctuary! The sanctity of the Gerizim cultus is the major theological issue which distinguishes the Samaritans, and which marks the Testament as a Samaritan work. The Samaritan theological point of view is also represented in the Testament in the understanding of Moses as Religionsstifter, and of Joshua as founder of the First Kingdom and successor of Moses. The prophets of Israel and Judah (i.e., those recognized in the Jewish canon) do not figure in this account; it is Moses alone who is the prophet of God. Chapters 2-8 of the Testament present a view of history consistent with the Samaritan Geschichtsbild: the account begins with a schism (the Eli schism) and continues with a brief account of the history of two groups of tribes down to the Babylonian exile. The ten tribes represent the apostate, schismatic part of the Israelite nation; the two tribes represent the faithful people of God with a legitimate sanctuary. But these two divisions do not represent the kingdoms of Judah and Israel, as those who know only Jewish traditions might suspect. The two faithful tribes are Ephraim and Manasseh, loyal to the Gerizim sanctuary; the ten apostate tribes are Judah and Benjamin of the south and the other eight tribes of the north! In this, Haacker follows a tradition preserved in Macdonald's Chronicle II, that eight of the ten tribes of the north followed Jeroboam in his apostasy, and that the tribes of Ephraim and Manasseh alone remained loyal to Yahweh and his sanctuary.[61]

---

60. K. H. Haacker, "Assumptio Mosis - eine samaritanische Schrift?" Theologische Zeitschrift, 25 (1969), 385-405.

61. Ibid., 400-401. It should be noted, however, that the so-called Chronicle II is essentially a chronistic account following the outline of the Jewish historical books, with extensive editing according to Samaritan traditions. In this, the Samaritans have been desirous of disassociating themselves from any apostasy in northern Israel in ancient times to which Jewish historical sources bear witness!

The theme of T.M. 2:3-3:3 is that the judgment of God will be brought upon all Israel because of the sin of the ten tribes. In the exile (3:4-14), the ten tribes will be repentant because of the reproach of the two tribes (Ephraim and Manasseh), and acknowledge that what had befallen them was that of which Moses had earlier warned. (Deut. 32) After the return from exile, Jerusalem will be rebuilt (4:7), but the members of the two tribes (Ephraim and Manasseh again) will be sorrowful because they will be unable to offer sacrifices (4:8). The history of the two groups is then traced through the time of the Hasmoneans (5:1-6:1) and King Herod (6:2-6) to the event of Varus' partial destruction of the Jerusalem temple in 4 B.C.E. (6:8), and then to the culmination of Roman oppression under Hadrian (8:1-5). This last account is preceded by an anti-Rabbinic polemic (chap. 7). The work is to be dated ca. 135-138 C.E. Haacker offers no identification from Samaritan sources of the Taxo-figure of T.M. 9:1-7.[62]

It is an ingenious tour de force which Haacker has offered. In this, everything hangs on the correct identification of the two and ten tribes. That these were the kingdoms of Judah and Israel, and not the divisions suggested by Haacker, seems more likely to be the case, and would involve less strain in the interpretation of the Testament. As for the theological understanding of Moses and Joshua, these were (as we have noted above) characteristic of at least one circle of Samaritan thought. There is no reason to maintain, however, that such views were the exclusive property of Samaritan theologians. If the Testament of Moses was a Jewish writing (as almost all of its commentators claim it was), it was representative of a particular school of Jewish thought which shared much in common with Samaritanism, especially that branch of the Samaritan faith which magnified Joshua as well as Moses. It is not difficult to explain the similarities in detail between the Testament and the Asaṭir. It may have been that both documents were dependent upon a common testament-pattern for Moses' last address. It may have been that the author of the Asaṭir knew the Testament of Moses, or, conversely, that the author of the Testament knew an early Samaritan work of which the medieval Asaṭir is a late witness. It is not likely that the Testament of Moses is a Samaritan writing.

---

62. There is a figure known from Samaritan sectarian history whose biography contains at least one element in common with Taxo. That is Dusis (Dositheus), the contemporary of Simon Magus, who was said by Abu'l Fatḥ to have died a martyr's death by voluntary starvation in a cave. His death resulted in a sectarian movement among the Samaritans through the activity of his disciple Levi. This tradition of the martyrdom of Dositheus is attested also by Epiphanius. Montgomery, Samaritans, pp. 256-258.

THREE ARMENIAN ACCOUNTS OF THE DEATH OF MOSES

Michael E. Stone

The Hebrew University of Jerusalem

The three texts presented here deal with the death of Moses, as it was viewed in the Armenian Church tradition. No attempt is made here to analyse this material; it is simply presented as source material for the further investigation of these traditions.

1. The Biblical Paraphrases

This extensive narrative text which deals with Biblical history from Enoch down to Solomon is largely composed of a mosaic of Biblical verses and fragments of verses, to which certain apocryphal traditions have been added. It will be published in the forthcoming Armenian Apocrypha from Unpublished Manuscripts (Apocrypha Veteris Testamenti in Lingua Armeniaca Conservata, Vol. I), Jerusalem: Israel Academy of Sciences and Humanities and St. James Press [in press]. Not all the text given here is translated in full in that volume. Biblical references indicate dependence, not necessarily quotation.

The two manuscripts are:

A   Erevan, Matenadaran 3854, 1471 C.E. (Catalogue, I, cols. 1097-98).

B   Erevan, Matenadaran 423 lm, xv cent. (Catalogue, I, col. 1175).

And at that time there was neither book nor law. Book and law were those ten commandments which Moses brought. And the Lord said to Moses,

"The day of your death has arrived." (Deut. 31:14)

And Moses, the servant of God died (ibid, 34:5; B omits), and they buried him (ibid, 6;A) [And the angel buried him (B)]. Moses was 120 years old when he died (ibid 7).

2. The Vita of Moses

This text, which appears as the Life of Moses in one cycle of the Armenian version of Vitae Prophetarum will be published in the same volume as the preceding.

The manuscript is:

H   Erevan, Matenadaran 1500, 1271-1288 C.E. (Catalogue,I, col. 568)

The angel of the Lord came to Moses and said,

"I know that you have learned many earthly things. Now <the time> has come upon you to return to the earth whence you were taken."

The prophet answered weeping and said,

"Oh! Ask this body if it abandons this soul."

The angel reprimanded him and said,

"You abandon the Lord's counsel."

The prophet said,

"My mouth spoke with God and my eyes saw the light of the Godhead and my nostrils smelt the fragrance of sweetness and my ears heard the word of the redeemer and the voice of the holy spirit, and how do you take my soul?"

And the angel said,

"Come to Mount Nebo."

And he went with him. And he said,

"Open your mouth!"

and with the opening (i.e. of his mouth) he gave up his ghost. And he said,

"Oh, for the heavenly things are sweeter than honeycomb."

3. The History of Moses

This text was published by S. Yovsēp'ianc', <u>Ankanon Girk' Hin Ktakaranac</u> (<u>Uncanonical Writings of the Old Testament</u>), Venice: Mechitarist Fathers, 1898, pp. 199-206. The material translated here is found on pages 204 - 206. A previous, unsatisfactory English translation was prepared by J. Issaverdens, <u>Uncanonical Writings of the Old Testament</u>, Venice: Mechitarist Fathers, 1934 (2 ed.), pp. 133-140.

And Moses appointed Joshua son of Nun as leader of Israel in his stead, and he himself ascended to the peak of Mt. Nebo.

And there Moses died at the age of 120. His eyes were not dimmed nor his cheeks withered, for Moses' face was illumined by the epiphany of God, like the brightness of the future life, and that which Adam had in the Garden, so that the children of Israel could not look upon him except for Aaron and Joshua. Therefore the children of Israel placed seven veils upon Moses' face, and then they could speak with him. And Moses had no beard on account of the bright shining of his face.

He desired to see Jerusalem and the other holy places and God did not grant him permission, for he had angered the Lord over the waters of disputation, for this reason. Miriam, Moses' sister, who was a virgin and a prophet had died and Moses was in mourning and the people were thirsty. They murmured against God and disputed with (complained against) Moses. Therefore Moses went sadly and struck the rock angrily. ⟨This was his sin⟩ for he should have struck the rock humbly and with prayer, as was his custom to do on other days, and not with anger. For this reason God did not permit him to see the promised land, but said to him to go to Mount Nebo and to see the land of Jerusalem from there, and to die there on the peak of Mount Nebo, near the house of the idols of Peor, opposite Jericho, on the far side of the Jordan.

Michael, the archangel, buried him and no man knew his tomb and his bones up to the present, for two reasons. First, because Moses was named God. Therefore he was buried secretly and unknown to men, lest they see their God dead. Second, lest men take his tomb and bones as an object of worship. From there was no prophet from Israel like Moses, whom God knew face to face, through signs and wonders which he did through him.

The children of Israel bewailed Moses in Araboth Moab, opposite Jericho, for thirty days, no more and no less. For thirty days is the number <of days of the cycle> of the moon, and then it is born anew and indicates our rising from the dust and renewal to immortality.

Moses the prophet underwent four births<s>: the first, of his mother, the second, of water, the third of fire when he remained with God on the peak of Mt. Sinai for forty days in the fire, and then he was born of the fire. Moses' fourth birth was of the rock when God placed him in the fissure of the rock, when he saw God's back, and there Moses was born as a son of rock.

Moses fasted for three forty day periods corresponding to the number of his years, a day for each year, for the years of his life were three times forty which makes one hundred and twenty.

No-one was found like him in all the generations and among all the prophets of Israel, for he spoke with God mouth to mouth. His perfect resurrection has taken place, for after being resurrected he came to Tabor as a witness to the divinity of Jesus Christ, son of Mary.

Final Note

These and similar Armenian pseudepigraphs on occasion preserve rather old traditions and extremely interesting formulations of extant and otherwise known material. It is hoped that making these translations available will contribute to the advance of the study of the Moses traditions.

Michael E. Stone
Department of the History of
 Jewish Thought
The Hebrew University of
 Jerusalem

THE ASCENSION OF MOSES AND THE HEAVENLY JERUSALEM
translated by Harold W. Attridge
Harvard University

Introduction

This haggadic midrash is taken from the eleventh century Bereshit Rabbati, which is attributed to Moshe HaDarshan and which contains much earlier material. Parts of this midrash were included in the Pugio Fidei of the thirteenth century Spanish polemicist Raymundus Martinus.[1] Otherwise Bereshit Rabbati survives in a single Hebrew manuscript. The portion of the MS containing our midrash was published by Jellinek[2] and subsequently with notes by A. Epstein.[3] Finally the whole MS of Bereshit Rabbati was published with an introduction and extensive notes by Ch. Albeck.[4] That edition served as the basis for the text published by J. Ebn-Shmuel[5] in a collection of apocalyptic midrashim with some introductory material. The text of Ebn-Shmuel's edition has been translated here and his lineation has been maintained, as indicated by the slashes (/). Biblical passages have been rendered according to the RSV except where the context requires another translation. Such exceptions have been noted.

Text

"This is none other than the house of God" (Gen.28:17)./ Our rabbis said: The very day that the death of Moses, our teacher, drew near, the Holy One,/ Blessed be He, raised him up to the heavens on high and showed him his reward and what was destined to be.

5   The divine attribute of Mercy stood before Moses, our teacher - peace be upon him - and said to him, "I proclaim to you good tidings,/ in which you will rejoice. Turn your face toward the throne of mercy and see!" He turned his face toward/ the throne of mercy and saw the Holy One,

---

[1] Raymundi Martini Pugio fidei adversus Mauros et Judaeos cum observationibus Josephi de Voisin, et introductione Jo. Benedicti Carpzovi (Leipzig 1687). Cf. also S. Libermann, Shkiin, a few words on some Jewish legends, customs and literary sources found in Karaite and Christian works. 2nd ed. (Jerusalem; Wahrmann 1970).

[2] A. Jellinek, Bet ha-Midrasch, 3rd ed. (Jerusalem; Wahrmann 1967), Vol. VI, pp. xxii-xxiii.

[3] In A. Epstein, Eldad ha-Dani, seine Berichte über die X Stämme und deren Ritus (Pressburg; Alkalay 1891), pp. 69-70.

[4] Ch. Albeck, Midrash Bereshit Rabbati, ex libro R. Mosis Haddarshan collectus e codice pragensi cum adnotationibus et introductione, 2nd ed. (Jerusalem; Mekize Nirdamim 1967) pp. 136-137.

[5] Judah Ebn-Shmuel, Midrashe Ge'ulah, 2nd ed. (Jeruslaem; Bialik Institute 1954), pp. 14-22.

Blessed be He, building the Temple with precious stones/ and
pearls, and between each stone was the splendour of the
Shekinah, which is more precious than pearls; and Messiah/ Son
of David was standing in its midst and Aaron, his brother, was
standing up wearing his cloak.

10 Aaron spoke/ with Moses, "At this time do not touch me,
for because of the Shekinah I fear for you, for/ man should
not enter here before he tastes of death and delivers his soul
to the angel of death."/

When he heard Aaron's words, he fell on his face before
the Holy One, Blessed be He, and said to Him,/ "Master of the
Universe, permit me to speak with your Messiah before I die."

The Holy One,/ Blessed be He, said to Michael, "Go and
teach him my great Name, so that the flame of the Shekinah
shall not consume him."

15 When Messiah Son of David and Aaron, his brother, saw him,
they understood that the Lord had taught him His great Name/
and they rose before him, Messiah and Aaron, and they said to
him,/ "Blessed be He who enters in the Name of the Lord"
(Ps. 118:26)./

Moses asked Messiah Son of David, "The Holy One, Blessed
be He, spoke to me and said He would build the Temple/ on
earth, the Temple for Israel, and now shall I see Him building
20 the Temple/ with His own hand in heaven?!"

Messiah said to Moses, "Moses, Jacob, your father, saw
the House that will be built/ on earth and he saw the House
which the Holy One, Blessed be He, will build with His own
hand in heaven and he understood/ fully that the House which
the Holy One, Blessed be He, will build with His own hand in
heaven with precious stones/ and pearls and the splendour of
the Shekinah, that is the Temple which will stand for Israel
for ever/ and ever until the end of all generations.

"Thus He said on the night in which he (Jacob) slept on
25 the stone and saw/ Jerusalem built on earth and Jerusalem
built in heaven and the Holy One, Blessed be He,/ appeared to
Jacob, our ancestor, standing. He spoke to Jacob, 'Jacob, My
son, at this time I stand above you until/ your sons take their
stand before Me;' - for it is said, ' The Lord stood above
him' (Gen. 28:13),[1]/ and of Israel it is said, 'and

---

[1] RSV "above it"

they took their stand at the foot of the mountain' (Ex.19:17), and it says,/ 'You all stand here today' (Dt. 29:9).

30 "When Jacob saw one Jerusalem on earth and another/ in heaven, he said, 'This one on earth is nothing - for it is said, 'Not this, but rather the house/ of God' (Gen. 28:17)[2] - A Temple which will stand for my children for generations of generations is not this one but rather that Temple/ which He builds with His own hands,' and if you see the Holy One, Blessed be He, building a Temple for Himself/ in heaven with His own hands, in the same fashion with His own hands will He build it on earth, for it is said, 'The Temple,[3]/ O Lord, which Thy hands have established' (Ex. 15:17)."/

35 When Moses, our teacher - peace be upon him - heard these words from the mouth of Messiah/ Son of David, he rejoiced greatly and he looked towards the Holy One, Blessed be He, and said to Him,/ "Master of the Universe, when will this Jerusalem which is built descend below?"

The Holy One, Blessed be He, said to him,/ "I have not related this time to any creature, neither to the first ones nor to the last ones;/ shall I relate it to you?!"

He said to Him, "Master of the Universe, grant me an indication from the events."

The Holy One, Blessed be He, said/ to him, "I shall scatter Israel first with a winnowing fan throughout the gates
40 of the earth/ and they shall be dispersed to the four corners of the world among all nations and by them that verse will be fulfilled which is written thus,/ 'If your outcasts are in the uttermost parts of heaven, from there the Lord your God will gather you, and from there/ He will fetch you' (Dt. 30:4). And I shall extend my hand as yet a second time and gather those who were with Johanan ben Qareaḥ to/ the land of Pathros and those who shall be in the land of Shinar and Hamath and Elam and Cush, for it is said,/ 'On that day the Lord will extend His hand yet a second time to recover the remnant which is
45 left/ of His people, from Assyria, from Egypt, from Pathros, from Ethiopia, from Elam, from Shinar, from Hamath,/ and from the islands of the sea.' (Is. 11:11)."/

---

[2] RSV "This is none other than the house of God." The midrashic manipulation of the verse which follows demands the translation given in the text.

[3] RSV "sanctuary"

At that time Moses descended from heaven rejoicing, and the
angel of death descended after him,/ and he did not give his
spirit and his soul to the angel until the Holy One, Blessed be
He, showed him His face/ and he gave his soul to the Holy One,
Blessed be He, with whole heart and willing soul.

Textual Apparatus

It should be noted that the English apparatus is slightly
different from that of Ebn-Shmuel's edition. One item not
mentioned by Ebn-Shmuel has been included. Some of the material
has been rearranged for greater conciseness and clarity and some
of Ebn-Shmuel's comments have been condensed.

Sigla
B. Bereshit Rabbati MS, from the library of the Prague community,
   as published in Albeck
P. Pugio Fidei
P^{var} A MS variant of the Pugio Fidei, as recorded by Albeck.
E. Epstein   J. Jellinek
A. Albeck   S. Ebn-Shmuel

3   Our rabbis said B: Our teacher Joshua ben Nun said P.
10   Text punctuated thus by Ebn-Shmuel: Aaron spoke with Moses at
     this time, "Do not touch me" EA
10f do not . . . for you B: Moses, do not come near because the
     Shekinah is here. I fear for you because of it P.
12   When . . . Blessed be He S (cf. lines 35-36): He fell on his
     face before the Holy One, Blessed be He, when he heard the
     words of Aaron B.
14   to Michael added by S.
14f Go . . . consume him B: "Go!" and He taught him His great Name
     so that the flame of the Shekinah should not consume him P: Go
     and learn with Aaron, your brother, the letters of My great
     Name, so that the fire of the flame of the Shekinah may not
     consume you P^{var}.
15   Aaron his brother om P^{var}.
18f He would . . . for Israel JS: The Holy One, Blessed be He,
     will build the Temple on earth, He will build (and He will
     build A) for Israel B: The Holy One, Blessed be He, will build
     the Temple on earth for Israel P.
19   and now P: and soB: and here A.
22   with precious stones and ES: both with precious stones and B.
25   The Holy One . . . spoke to Jacob S: and he (Moses A) saw
     standing above Jacob our father and the Holy One, Blessed be
     He, spoke to Jacob B. A understands this to mean At the time
     when the Messiah was speaking Moses saw this picture, namely
     that Jacob was standing and the Holy One, Blessed be He, spoke
     to him, "Jacob, my son, etc."
28   and of Israel it is said S: and Israel B.
28   and it says S: B omits.
30   he said A: and he said B.
31   God S: B omits.
33   in heaven PA: B omits.
35   from the mouth of P: by virtue of JE: in the presence of B.
42   Johanan ben Qareah ES: Jonah ben Amatai B, A reading B
     declares it to be incomprehensible.
43   and Cush S: and Cush, etc B.
49   B adds at the end, Behold this is none other than the house of
     God.

www.ingramcontent.com/pod-product-compliance
Lightning Source LLC
Chambersburg PA
CBHW032004080426
42735CB00007B/505